WALKING
CANALS

Edited by
RONALD RUSSELL

DAVID & CHARLES
Newton Abbot   London   North Pomfret (Vt)

The editor and publishers wish to emphasise that walkers should gain permission from the owner before entering any private property.

British Library Cataloguing in Publication Data

Walking canals.
1. Canals — England   2. England — Description and travel — Guide-books
I. Russell, Ronald
914.2'0485'8   HE436.E/

ISBN 0-7153-8350-7

Typeset by ABM Typographics Ltd, Hull and printed in Great Britain by Redwood Burn Limited, Trowbridge, Wilts. for David & Charles (Publishers) Limited Brunel House   Newton Abbot   Devon

Published in the United States of America by David & Charles Inc North Pomfret   Vermont 05053   USA

CONTENTS

FOREWORD

'Trespassers will be prosecuted.' This curt message still appears on a few old signs alongside the Board's towing paths, a grim reminder of a past era. Today, walkers are welcome on our towing paths and on many of those owned by other authorities.

Since the Board's inception we have been bedevilled by lack of money. We have been unable to maintain our canals, tunnels and reservoirs to a proper standard, and so few funds have been available to repair and improve our towing paths that the public must accept them as they find them. Some are overgrown, others are eroded, but many provide an easy and pleasant way into our waterways world, into the living past. You will be walking on paths built for a purpose, on routes enlivened by passing boats and busy locks. You will encounter fine old industrial buildings (canals in towns bring a special reward) and you will be refreshed at the public houses that once served the needs of the working boatmen. Heron, swan, mallard, perhaps a kingfisher, will be your companions.

The Board encourages walkers to its towing paths and so I welcome Ronald Russell's book of canalside walks. Such a book needed to be written; it is appropriate that it should have been compiled by an author with a vast knowledge of the inland, waterways.

Make the most of your waterways. Come walking where others have walked for more than 200 years. Like the canals themselves, the towing paths have gained a new purpose: the pleasure and recreation of the community that owns them.

Sir Frank Price, DL,
Chairman, British Waterways Board 1968–83

INTRODUCTION

The days when one could walk as one pleased through the countryside are, alas, over—if indeed they ever really existed. Probably there were always points of conflict between walkers and landowners but as cities and towns have grown and common land has shrunk, with more and more acres yielding to the plough, so the freedom of movement has been restricted. Leisure time has meanwhile increased and there is a growing awareness of the recreational value of the open air. One consequence of this is the guided or directed walk, for example, the Pennine Way, the Ridgeway or Offa's Dyke Path. It can be argued that the signposting and popularising of these routes could eventually lead to the destruction of that which they are intended to preserve, as they become overcrowded, trodden down and strewn with litter. There is a risk of this happening, but the real destruction stems from the builder or the farmer with his plough; what they do is usually irreversible.

Through much of our countryside and many of our towns and cities, however, run some two thousand miles of pathway which, as far as we can tell, are likely to remain inviolate. The towing paths of our canals were created to be walked along. By their very nature they lead you through the history of the Industrial Revolution, along the routes travelled by the coal that fuelled the factories, the iron, steel, bricks and timber from which its artefacts were created, and the grain, cheese and produce that fed the growing population, linking London with Birmingham, Leeds with Liverpool, the Trent with the Mersey, the industrial North and Midlands with the Thames. They take you through areas of city and countryside otherwise inaccessible; and as you walk the water accompanies you, almost still in the long pounds, lively by the locks, reflecting light and sound.

With the few exceptions of canals which have been long abandoned and dewatered, you do not need a printed guide to help you walk along a towpath. Your path is clear; you cannot mistake it and if you fall off you will only get your feet wet. The walks that follow in Part II tell you not so much where to go as what to look out for; each walk is described by an enthusiast who knows both the area and the history of the particular canal. No claim is made that these are the best canalside walks, only that they are all good ones.

The majority of the walks are between four and twelve miles in length so that each can be completed in a single outing. For those who wish to devote a weekend, or even a whole week, to canal walking, there are outline descriptions of three longer walks through beautiful and varied countryside with plenty of places where you can obtain overnight accommodation. You can, of course, pitch a tent but not, please, on the towpath itself.

The descriptions of the walks have been arranged in alphabetical order of canal—as no better method of presenting them suggested itself—with the three longer walks at the end. Many walkers will use public transport to get them to and from their routes and I strongly recommend obtaining the 'Principal Bus Links' map from the National Bus Company, 25 New Street Square, London EC4A 3AP, and the British Rail Passenger Network map as well.

Finally, I should like to express my gratitude to the contributors and to all those who in turn helped them, walking with them making observations and notes or answering their questions and guiding them on their way. My thanks also go to Sir Frank Price for his Foreword and my best wishes to the members and staff of the British Waterways Board and to all the officers and workers of the canal voluntary societies for their efforts to maintain and improve our towpath walks.

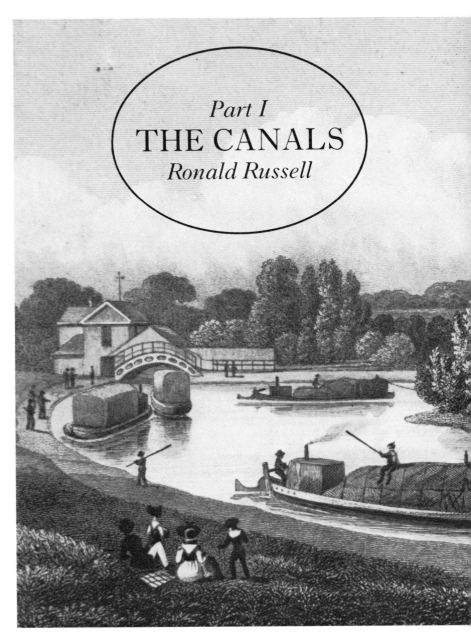

Part I
THE CANALS
Ronald Russell

The towpath at Paddington, 1828 *(engraved by S. Lacey after a drawing by Thomas H. Shepherd)*

1
THE TOWPATH

Jem Ford is the hero of one of the very few tales of canal life, *The Old Lock Farm* by Annie Gray, published in the 1880s. Little Jem Ford could tell us the truth about canal life:

> Jem could tell us of wild weird tracks of land, miles from here, through which canals must wend their weary way; of rough and crowded wharves piled with coal-heaps, timber, sacks of corn, and what not; wharves made horrible oftentimes by the incessant flow of bad language which falls from the lips of all too many of the men and women who spend their lives on the water. He could remind us that it is not always summer, and that the sun is not always shining; that in rain and in hail, in wind and in snow, in the depth of winter as in the height of summer, weary feet must traverse long miles of tow-path by the side of the patient horse, stumble over frozen ridges, and splash through mud and clay.

The reference to bad language indicates that the story was essentially a tract; it was published by the Sunday School Union and its views were strongly influenced by the reformer George Smith. Nevertheless Jem's reminder of the weary feet traversing long miles of towpath by the side of the patient horse is illuminating to those of us who have never seen a horse-drawn boat and associate towpaths more with patient fishermen than with the patient horse.

The towpaths were built at the same time as the canals, along one bank only (except in a few instances in the later years of canal construction) and were as far as possible continuous. Here and there you will find a bridge so narrow that it spans only the water channel, but clearly this created inconvenience and the usual practice was to carry the bridge over the towpath as well. On almost all canals towing by horse—or possibly by mule or donkey—was undertaken from the beginning, unlike river navigations where vessels either sailed or, when this was impossible, were bow-hauled by gangs of men. John Phillips in his

History of Inland Navigation notes this special advantage of canals, remarking that at Barton on the Bridgewater Canal, 'We may, at the same time, see seven or eight stout fellows labouring like slaves to drag a boat slowly up the river Irwell, and one horse drawing two or three boats on the canal, which is carried over the river at this place like a magnificent Roman aqueduct.' These stout fellows were notorious for their riotous behaviour, not surprising considering the nature of their employment. Overtaking was usually forbidden with horse-towing and, when travelling in opposite directions, unladen boats dropped their towlines so that loaded boats would not lose way. Perhaps it was false economy to construct towpaths on one bank only in view of the wear and tear on the single path and the problems created when fast passenger boats were used, but canal companies were generally loth to spend more than seemed essential when purchasing land for the cutting of a canal and a second towpath must have seemed a needless luxury.

As horse-towing declined, it was no longer necessary to keep the towpath in good condition, and the turbulence and wash caused by the increased speed of powered boats gave rise to the problem of wear on canal banks. Working boatmen, under the pressures of time and money, sometimes showed little regard for the 'track'; modern pleasure boaters, however, have no excuse and the observant walker alongside the more popular canals can easily see the consequences of excessive use of the throttle. In places the towpath may be almost worn away and you will sometimes see lengths of piling isolated in the channel where the infilling behind them has been sucked away by the frequent passage of boats. Modern piling is usually of steel; but it is interesting as you walk to look for the materials used in earlier years. There may be stone pitching, camp shedding (piles and planks), old railway sleepers or simply beds of rushes. Concrete and sheets of corrugated material are serviceable but less picturesque.

In recent years many miles of towpath in towns have been excavated to provide routes for high-pressure gas grids or electricity cables and, in Birmingham, for the pipelines of British Oxygen. The surfaces are usually relaid with substantial concrete blocks; this improvement of the towpath of the Regent's Canal was the first step towards the creation of the now popular canalside walk. City towpaths make fascinating walks. Not only London and Birmingham, but also Manchester, Liverpool, Leeds, Stoke-on-Trent, Worcester and Bath seem to gain an extra dimension when seen from the towpath. Lewis Braithwaite's *Canals in Towns* makes an excellent guide to the exploration of cities from the canal bank and gives brief details of the special qualities of each walk. Canal routes take you through areas inaccessible in any other way and this applies even when the canal itself has been closed and dewatered. The walk along the line of the Wiltshire & Berkshire Canal through Swindon is a good example and presents no difficulties of access. Some attempts are more demanding: try, for example, to trace the course of the Glamorganshire Canal through Cardiff —at first it may seem to have disappeared entirely—or the Bradford Canal, 3½ miles from Shipley on the Leeds & Liverpool Canal to Forster Square in the centre of Bradford.

Contrary to what is sometimes thought, the British Waterways Board, the guardian of most of our canals, actively encourages towpath walking and points out that the public has complete freedom to walk the towpaths—taking them as they find them. As the towpath is an essential part of the navigation, the Board's staff do have discretion to prevent public access when necessary on towpaths over which there is no public right of way, as might happen during reconstruction or repair work, but this is likely to mean only a short diversion. If you wish to walk the towpaths of the commercial navigations, however, it is advisable to make enquiries beforehand and not take the right of access for granted. Commercial waterways controlled by the British Waterways Board are as follows:

Aire & Calder Navigation
Calder & Hebble Navigation
Caledonian Canal
Crinan Canal
Sheffield & South Yorkshire Navigation
New Junction Canal
Trent Navigation
Weaver Navigation and Weston Canal
River Severn (Stourport – Gloucester)
Gloucester & Sharpness Canal
River Lee Navigation

The legal position concerning the maintenance of towpaths is not completely clear. According to the authors of the 1974 Fraenkel Report on the operation and maintenance of the waterways, 'it appears to be generally accepted that, in consequence of the Transport Act, 1968, the BWB are no longer under an obligation to maintain the towing paths of their waterways so that, by implication, no one has cause for complaint if a towing path falls into disuse or becomes impassable because of erosion or growth of vegetation.' However, the Report goes on to say, having examined what happens in practice, that 'while the Board do not recognise any statutory obligation to maintain the towing paths in connection with navigation, they nevertheless regard them as integral parts of the waterways and therefore deserving of maintenance in order that they may function satisfactorily.' The Report agrees with the Board's general practice, 'that their responsibilities in this respect are on the same footing as for other structural components of the system', and continues by commenting that maintenance should therefore be directed to at least the following:

Securing continuous and ready means of access on foot or bicycle to all parts of the waterway for inspection

Obtaining access for labour and mobile plant engaged on routine maintenance operations such as grass mowing, hedge trimming and ditch clearance: also land-based dredging

Providing for passage on foot or bicycle for preparation of locks, access to moorings etc

Where appropriate, for the accommodation of horse or tractor engaged in the towage of dumb cruising and/or maintenance craft

Angling and other amenity and environmental pursuits

Finally the Report says that 'where adequate bank protection exists, or the waterside verge is sound, a satisfactory towing path will in general be obtained if the clear width is not less than 2m and the surface is reasonably level, draining either to the waterway or to a lateral ditch,' adding that where towing paths are public rights of way a higher standard of maintenance, to which the local authority may agree to contribute, might be called for. You will, of course, quickly discover that very many lengths of towpath are nothing like 2m (6ft 6in) wide and that cycling on the towpath has become one of the more hazardous means of progress. Lock-wheeling (cycling ahead to prepare the locks for your boat), once a popular time-saving method for working boat crews, is now seldom practised, and on parts of the Oxford and Shropshire Union canals it is sometimes difficult to discern the towpath at all. But do remember that it is lack of cash, not lack of will, that is the reason, a point appreciated by some canal societies whose members voluntarily take on the task of towpath clearance and surface maintenance.

In the mid-nineteenth century it is estimated that there were about four thousand miles of towpath in England and Wales with a further three hundred miles in Scotland. Over a quarter of this total has been lost and many continuous routes have been broken. What is left amounts to about one-fortieth of the total footpath mileage in England and Wales. These figures include river navigations and it is these that account for a good proportion of the lost mileage. In particular, sections of towpath along the Thames and the Severn have disappeared. The Regional Water Authorities, who are responsible for most river navigations, have no legal responsibility to maintain the towpaths, which themselves generate no revenue. However, most of the longer towpath stretches which are established as public rights of way are alongside rivers, with 74 miles along the Thames, 67 miles along the Trent and 34 miles along the Nene. Many lengths are in private ownership and the legal position is frequently obscure. What is clear is that there is enormous potential for establishing long- and middle-distance footpath routes by combining canal and river towpaths. A Water Space Amenity Commission Report, published in 1977, acknowledged this potential and recommended 'as a matter of some urgency' the setting up of a working party to 'examine the problems of providing public access to towpaths and to make recommendations about the establishment of a national system of towpath walks'. This is not likely to happen in an unfavourable economic climate, but agreement on a national policy would help to ensure that further mileage is not lost and that the future of what remains is assured.

If you are seriously concerned about the condition of a particular length of towpath, it is worth discussing the matter with the local office of the British Waterways Board and finding

Picnicking on the bank of the Market Harborough arm of the Grand Union
Canal *(British Waterways Board)*

out whether there are plans for improvement. Some (but not all) local authorities are interested in the canals within their area and it may be worth contacting the appropriate official. The Inland Waterways Association or local canal society may also be willing to make representations on your behalf. Do not be afraid to make your views known; indeed, as a taxpayer you have a right to do so. That some of our waterways survive at all is due to the concern and involvement of individuals and voluntary bodies and you should be as concerned about the preservation of the towpaths as members of the Ramblers' Association are about footpaths across the countryside.

2
WALKING THROUGH TIME

It is the walker rather than the boater who can best appreciate the problems that faced the surveyors and engineers of the canal line. From the towpath, the map comes to life; the demands imposed by the contours of the land are clear and the reasons for locks, embankments, cuttings and aqueducts become obvious. It is possible to guess the age of the canal from the way in which its engineer has attempted to solve the problems of construction. The canal which tries as far as possible to follow natural contours, with single locks at irregular intervals, insignificant cuttings and embankments and narrow tunnels with sometimes little cover, is likely to have been built before 1790; for example, the Trent & Mersey and much of the Oxford Canal before the straightening of the 1830s, which took eleven miles out of the forty-four mile length between Hawkesbury and Napton. In contrast, the canal line with locks grouped together in flights or staircases, and with straight stretches carried on long embankments or in deep cuttings, will be of later construction; examples include the main line of the Shropshire Union and the Macclesfield Canal. With a couple of exceptions, only the later tunnels were built with permanent towpaths, like the later Newbold Tunnel on the North Oxford Canal and Netherton Tunnel on the Birmingham Canal Navigations, opened in 1858; these two tunnels had the added luxury of a towpath on either side.

Of the earlier eighteenth-century canals, the St Helen's, or Sankey Brook Navigation, completed in 1759 was finally abandoned in 1963. Some of it has been obliterated, although several stretches can still be walked (see *Lancashire Waterways* by Gordon Biddle). The Bridgewater Canal, opened from Worsley to Manchester in 1765 and later extended to Runcorn and to Leigh, is, apart from Runcorn Locks, still in operation and around Worsley and Lymm in particular makes interesting walking. The most characteristic of the earlier canals, however, is probably the Staffordshire & Worcestershire (1772). This canal retained its independence until the inland waterways were nationalised in 1948. Time has dealt kindly with the Staffordshire & Worcestershire which retains many of its original red brick bridges, several circular weirs and a fascinating collection of locks, including Compton Lock, the first narrow lock built by James Brindley, and the flight of three called The Bratch.

Among other earlier canals are the Droitwich, the Trent & Mersey, Chesterfield and Stroudwater. Of these, only the Trent & Mersey remains open throughout; the Droitwich and Stroudwater are both closed but are currently under restoration, and the upper section of the Chesterfield above Worksop has not been navigable since 1908. Two major canals that are still open, the Oxford and the Coventry, were also begun in this period although both of them took over twenty years to complete.

Rapidly developing industry and the demand for cheaper and more efficient transport of heavy goods led, as the eighteenth century neared its end, to an upsurge of interest in canals. Investors, encouraged by the profitability of the first canals, were quick to come forward, and between 1791 and 1795 forty-eight new canals were authorised. These included the Grand Junction, Worcester & Birmingham, Rochdale, Huddersfield, Nottingham, Stratford and Leicester canals, almost all the canals to be built in South Wales, the Kennet & Avon, the Gloucester & Berkeley, and a number of projects in the West-country and the Welsh Borders all of which, except the Somersetshire Coal Canal, were financial disasters. By the late 1790s, however, the boom was over; between 1798 and 1830 only twenty-four canals were initiated and with the 1840s the railways began their takeover.

The last main line canal—except for the rather different Manchester Ship Canal—was opened in 1842; this, the Chard Canal, survived for only twenty-four years. The subsequent story was of a diminishing network with sales, closures and abandonments recorded almost every year. Nevertheless, most of the canal system remains open and usable, and there are good prospects of reopening for many of the canals now closed, thanks to the efforts of the numerous voluntary restoration

societies that have been formed in recent years. On the waterways pleasure cruisers have taken over from commercial boats
and on some of the more popular stretches there are now more
boat movements in the summer than in the busiest days of commercial carrying.

What the walker will not fail to notice is the poor condition of
the canals even on these popular stretches. Do not think that
this is only a consequence of the economic recession of the early
1980s. It was, on the whole, an impoverished system that was
nationalised in 1948, and successive governments have shown
little enthusiasm for improving it. Ever since its inception, the
British Waterways Board has been the Cinderella of
nationalised transport undertakings and no Prince Charming
has ever appeared. In 1974 it was estimated that the cost of overtaking the arrears of maintenance amounted to £37,600,000 and
the annual cost of operating and maintaining the system was
reckoned to be £8,800,000. In the light of recent inflation, these
figures convey little. In the past few years there have been
several major bank breaches and tunnel closures which have
underlined the urgency to which the Fraenkel Report drew
attention. To deal with some of these disasters, the Govern-
ment increased the grant in aid for the year 1982/3, and if this is
a sign of a change of attitude it will be doubly welcome.

That the canals fulfil a demand can be seen from the figures
quoted in the British Waterways Board's Annual Report for
1981. In England and Wales there were over 22,000 private
pleasure boats using the canals and more than 2,000 hire boats
which gave holidays to an estimated 185,000 people. In
addition, there are hotel boats, trip boats, restaurant boats and
about twenty boats specially designed for the disabled. The
canals are popular with canoeists and are fished by some quarter
of a million anglers. 'Even more people use the towing paths for
walking,' says the Board, 'whether for a gentle stroll, an enjoyable short cut or a long-distance walk.' As amenities, our canals
are very cheap indeed.

With increasing age, however, the fragility of the canals and
their structures becomes more obvious. Insensitive patching
and repair work stands out starkly against mellow red brick or
handsome stone. There has been some tactful restoration,
notably on the Brecon & Abergavenny Canal and on the Slat-

tocks flight of the Rochdale Canal where the Manpower Services Commission provided the labour force, but this recent work on the Rochdale is in sharp contrast to the appalling treatment of the locks at Ancoats a few years ago, which reduced them to large shallow dustbins and won a civic award. The walker will be able to give his own awards for restoration work which respects what is there already, and produce his own catalogue of horrors. Some of the horrors are likely to be the responsibility of individual boatyards and hiring firms, whose brash advertising sometimes disfigures the waterside scene.

Understanding the significance of what you see, the reasons for the existence of various structures and the original purposes of the different canalside buildings adds enormously to the interest of your walk. A glance at the lie of the land explains the presence of locks, tunnels and aqueducts, and the many 'accommodation bridges' that do not carry public roads but are there because the canal cut through a farmer's fields and a bridge had to be provided to 'accommodate' him and facilitate the passage of his wagons or stock. Almost all overbridges also span the towpath, and the channel is often little wider than a lock. Where the towpath changes sides you will find turnover or roving bridges; as you cross you can work out for yourself how the design enabled the towing horse to cross without the towline having to be unhitched. Another unique design of bridge can be found at some of the locks on the Trent & Mersey, Staffordshire & Worcestershire and Southern Stratford canals, where the two halves of the span do not meet, leaving a gap for the towline to be passed through. Splendid Horseley Ironworks bridges carry the towpath over the entrances to the disused loops on the Oxford Canal; there are wooden lift bridges on the Southern Oxford, Llangollen, and Northampton arm of the Grand Union, and swing bridges on several canals, in particular on the Leeds & Liverpool. By many bridges, and by tunnels and aqueducts as well, you may find a stack of heavy stop planks used to drop into a pair of grooves in the canal banks, which you should find close by, and wedged tightly in to seal off a length of canal so that water could be drained away for repair or maintenance work.

Look out for evidence of the passage of horse-drawn boats on the structure of the bridges themselves. Frequently you will see

20

Ellesmere Tunnel on the Llangollen Canal *(British Waterways Board)*

deep grooves worn into the abutments by the towpath; often the brick or stonework has been protected by an iron guard or sometimes by wooden rollers. Bridge parapets may show similar grooves, caused by the friction of the towlines, as do bollards, especially beside and on the approaches to locks. On derelict and abandoned canals, these grooves are particularly eloquent.

More evidence of the horse-drawn traffic of the past can be found by some of the canalside pubs. In the mid-nineteenth century all these pubs would have had stabling for horses on overnight stops but much of this has disappeared or has been converted to other uses. The Swan at Fradley Junction could accommodate up to twenty-two horses, a very large number. More typical were The Boat at Gnosall and The Bridge at Audlem, which could each take eleven, while The King's Arms at Barbridge Junction could put up only four. The Broughton Arms at Rode Heath on the Trent & Mersey still preserves the wooden fittings in its stables, the old horse-trough and boatman's primitive lavatory. The top floor of the building incorporates two unlit and unheated boatmen's dormitories.

While some of the pubs still serve canal travellers, few of the surviving lock-cottages have kept their direct connection with the canal. Not that many survive; several, isolated and hence expensive to connect to main services, have been demolished in recent decades and only a handful, at flights of locks for example, still house a canal employee. Look out for these survivors. Many simply resemble other cottages of the locality, but the Southern Stratford retains six attractive single-storey cottages with roofs shaped like half-barrels, and on the Thames & Severn the five circular lengthsmen's cottages can still be found, three of them privately occupied. In places the cottages have long outlived the waterway as on the Leominster Canal where you can find four cottages and a handsome wharf-house although the canal itself has long been waterless and much of the bed obliterated. More unusual canal buildings include the fancy miniature castle by Hampstead Road Lock on the Regent's Canal, the round tower at Gailey on the Staffordshire & Worcestershire and the miniature Grecian temples on the Gloucester & Sharpness; these are bridge-keepers' cottages, each sited by one of the canal's swing bridges.

Other canalside structures include warehouses, offices and

other buildings associated with wharves. One of the finest complexes was at Ellesmere Port, but neglect, vandalism and a major fire in 1970 have destroyed much of Telford's creation. Shardlow on the Trent & Mersey and Stourport at the junction of the Severn and Staffordshire & Worcestershire have fine warehouses now converted into canal-associated uses. By almost every waterway you may find examples, from the utilitarian sheds of the Shropshire Union system to the handsome white-painted stone building now used as a boathouse at Llanfoist on the Brecon & Abergavenny Canal. Further south on this canal is a toll-house by the gauging stop at the end-on junction with the Monmouthshire Canal; toll-houses were built at almost all canal junctions but not many of them survive.

Wharves can be especially evocative if you are trying to summon up pictures of times past. At the beginning of this century, 22 wharves were in use on the 77 miles of the Oxford Canal; many of them have disappeared without trace, but the figure gives some indication of the business of the canal. Some were private, serving the factory or undertaking of their owner, but most were owned by the canal company and were available for public use. It is the remote wharves that are perhaps the most evocative; most distant of all must be Tyddyn, at the end of the Guilsfield Branch of the Montgomery Canal, or possibly Westonwharf at the termination of the disused Weston Branch of the Shropshire Union. Every waterside settlement had its wharf and where the canal line missed a village by a mile or two a wharf was usually built at the nearest convenient point and goods were transferred to wagons. The walker may be able to find evidence of such wharves where nothing is shown on the map; even modern canal maps tend to ignore wharf sites though a knowledge of their whereabouts can often help you to appreciate the canalscape.

Observing the variety of lock furniture and the different types of weirs adds to the interest of a towpath walk. Almost all the paddle gear needs a windlass to operate it, carried by the boat's crew, except in the case of manned locks. This deters vandalism and prevents waste of water. If you watch locks being worked, you will see that the simpler kinds of gear are usually the easiest to operate; enclosed ground paddles, as on the northern section of the Grand Union Canal, are not particularly

23

popular with those who turn the handle. Of all canals, the Leeds & Liverpool has the greatest variety of paddle gear and a voyage along this canal makes a series of different demands on the lock-worker's anatomy. Look out for additional paddles at certain locks, especially at flights or staircases, which connect with a side pond to save water. It is a pity that many side ponds are now disused; with the present labour shortage on the waterways they are likely to remain so. Fine examples can be found beside the Foxton flight on the Leicester arm of the Grand Union.

By many locks there are overfall or bypass weirs. These take off surplus water from the upper level which would otherwise pour over the lock-gates. They may be open waterfalls or slopes, smooth or stepped, brick culverts or circular as on the Staffordshire & Worcestershire Canal. There are also weirs where feeders join the canal, and waste weirs to run off excess water into a nearby stream. Weirs are essential to maintain water at the required level, guarding against flooding and the breaching of canal banks. To drain a length of canal, flood paddles may be used to run off the water; in early days these were sometimes installed in the canal bed like oversized bath plugs with chain attached.

Finally, look out for mileposts along the towpath. These were required by law so that tolls could be accurately estimated; sometimes half- and quarter-mile stages were also indicated. They may be stone, iron or a combination of both. Despite their weight and solidity, however, many have disappeared over the years. Occasionally you can find one in the undergrowth by the line of a derelict canal, and on the Montgomeryshire Canal sponsored mileposts are being installed as part of the fund raising so vital if this beautiful waterway is to be successfully restored to navigation. On some canals you may see boundary posts, perhaps in a field adjacent to the towpath, showing the boundary of the canal company's property. Many of these were erected by railway companies after they had taken over a particular canal, and the posts generally consist of bits of railway line.

Every structure associated with a canal had its special purpose. One of the chief pleasures of canalside walking is identifying these structures and working out, if it is not immediately apparent, what their purpose was.

3
BOATS AND THEIR CREWS

The variety of boats you can see when towpath walking today is quite astonishing. Restrictions on the size of boats are imposed by the dimensions of the particular canal: the length and breadth of the locks, the height of the lowest fixed bridge and the depth of the channel. Within these restrictions anything that floats goes, and a study of boats, whether moving or moored, adds colour and interest to your walk.

On the narrow canals of the Midlands the lock dimensions average 72ft x 7ft 2in and this dictated the size of the narrow boats that once traded on them, some of which survive today in their original form or converted to provide full living accommodation. The commercial narrow boats themselves varied according to the style of the boat-builder or the needs of the cargoes they carried. With the development of powered boating, the whole class became divided into those vessels which incorporated an engine—sometimes known as 'monkey-boats'—and those without, known as 'butties', which often provided living accommodation for the boatman and his family. Working in pairs, these were common sights on the canals in the second half of the nineteenth century and first half of the twentieth; if you are lucky you may see a working pair on the canals today, though there are very few of them about. The butty was a direct descendant of the horse-drawn boat of earlier years, possibly the last working example of which is the late Mr and Mrs Skinner's *Friendship* for years moored at Hawkesbury Junction and now in the Ellesmere Boat Museum.

The study of narrow boats is highly specialised. Several books have recently been written on this subject and you should read one or more of these if you want to increase your knowledge of canal boats. Paget-Tomlinson's *Britain's Canal and River Craft*, Smith's *Canal Boats and Boaters* and Chaplin's *The Narrow Boat Book* are some of the titles currently available.

Chaplin's *Short History of the Narrow Boat* is an inexpensive book that can easily be slipped into the pocket. Also useful and reasonably priced are some of the Robert Wilson publications which deal with the fortunes of various major canal carrying companies and with life on the canals in the first half of the twentieth century. If you find you are becoming a serious student of canal life, these little books (obtainable from canal shops, boatyards, the *Waterways World* book service or the Inland Waterways Association) will be essential to you; much of the information they contain is not available elsewhere.

The traditional colourful decoration of the narrow boat has made a strong appeal to the public imagination. The roses and castles have spread from the boats themselves to the decor of canalside pubs, souvenir shops, tourist literature, even tea towels. In the past, the boat painters were generally employed by the boatyards and it was often possible to tell from the style of the roses or castles where the boat had been painted—at Nurser's yard at Braunston, Tooley's at Banbury or the Poles-worth yard of Lees and Atkins. Unfortunately, exposed to wind and weather, painting on boat exteriors soon fades and flakes away and you will need to visit a museum to see examples of this older work.

Some of the narrow boats you will come across, whether conversions or purpose-built, may well be finely painted, perhaps by someone like Ron Hough who learned his craft at one of the old boatyards. Much modern work, however, is painted crudely by self-taught practitioners or, as on many hire boats, is the result of applied mass-produced transfers.

Narrow-boat decoration is by no means confined to roses and castles, which were mainly associated with the owner-captains of boats on the Grand Junction and Oxford canals. Geometrical designs, symbols from playing cards and characteristic signwriters' scrollwork can be seen on the strakes, the deck lid and cabin sides. On the large cabin side panel used to be painted the name of the owner or the carrying company to which the boat belonged—Fellows, Morton & Clayton; Samuel Barlow Coal Company; Grand Union Canal Carrying Company—with the boat's registration details above it. The lettering was derived from the style of late Victorian signwriting, with each letter blocked or shadowed in a second colour to give an impression of relief. On some boats efforts have been made to retain this traditional style, and occasionally an enthusiastic owner has his craft painted in the livery of the company for which it worked years ago. If, like many people, you become intrigued by the painted decoration of narrow boats you should obtain a copy of A. J. Lewery's *Narrow Boat Painting,* the only full study of the subject.

Narrow boats were also embellished with intricate decorative rope work and highly polished brass; the cabin interiors were rich with lace and pierced-edge hanging or ribbon plates, with more brass, roses and castles painted on doors and surfaces and much simulated wood grain. Water cans, hand bowls and dippers were also painted, predominantly with roses, as were the stools used inside the cabin. Many boat-owners today carry painted cans on their cabin roofs, but very few would wish to reproduce the cramped interior of the boat family's cabin.

Away from the narrow canals other types of craft were developed to suit the dimensions and characteristics of particular waterways. Outside museums, however, few of these craft survive. The best place to see the working survivors in any number is at the annual rally of the Inland Waterways Association held every August at a different venue on the canal system. It is especially fortunate if the venue is accessible by broad canal; then you may see the Humber keel *Comrade* and other vessels too broad-beamed to navigate narrow locks. On the Leeds & Liverpool Canal look out for a converted 'short boat' and on the Aire & Calder a train of compartment boats known as Tom Puddings. There is usually a good collection of barges on the Grand Union at Rickmansworth, and here and there you may see a canal tug or a carefully preserved committee boat, built for the directors of a canal company to make their annual inspection. The Boat Museum at Ellesmere Port has an extensive collection of inland-waterways craft.

Vessels specially designed for a certain type of waterway do not always perform well elsewhere. Narrow boats can be troublesome on natural rivers; they prove underpowered and unwieldy where there is likely to be much flow. Motor boats with high-revving engines are not suitable for canals, and lightweight craft can be troubled by side winds on narrow canals where there is little room to manoeuvre. Your walk will often be

27

enlivened by displays of eccentric boat-handling and you may be called on to catch a line or lend some muscle to help a boat away from the bank or off the mud. On the whole, canal users show high standards of courtesy and consideration and in this respect at least things may have improved since the old days.

Anyone whose awareness of the canal world is awakened will inevitably become curious about the ways and conditions of life of those who earned their livings by working boats on the canals. In the past few years, with the upsurge of interest in canals, efforts have been made to record the reminiscences and experiences of the old boatmen but there are not many at work in this field and it is always worth taking any opportunity of talking with an ex-boatman or lock-keeper. In this way, and by reading the specialist waterway magazines and such publications as Robert Wilson's *Life Afloat* you will be able to put together a reasonably detailed picture of canal life in the twentieth century. To go back earlier, however, is more difficult; it is surprising how little canal life attracted public attention in the nineteenth century and how sparse the published evidence seems to be. John Hollingsworth's series of three articles 'On the Canal' that appeared in Dickens' weekly *Household Words* in 1858 are now well known because they are the only full description by a journalist of a voyage on a working boat, incidentally providing the first printed evidence of canal-boat decoration. They share the magazine's pages with articles on 'Hindoo Law' and an account of a Chinese play, and seem just about as remote as these from the experience of the reading public. In 1874 there was an account in the *Illustrated London News* of the explosion of a gunpowder boat on the Regent's Canal and a page of woodcuts and an article in *The Graphic,* but not very much else.

Much of what is known about canal life in the earlier years comes from canal company records, parliamentary reports and the columns of local newspapers. Personal investigation was made by the social reformer George Smith of Coalville who described his efforts in his books *Our Canal Population* (1875) and *Canal Adventures by Moonlight* (1881). His campaign, directed at improving the living conditions of the boat people and providing education for their children, led to the Canal Boats Act of 1878 and its Amendment, requiring the registration and annual inspection of boats, in 1884. The picture painted by Smith was a grim one. 'Drunkenness, filthiness, and cruelty, selfish idleness at the cost of children and animals; thieving, fighting and almost every other abomination prevailed among them,' wrote Smith of the boat people of Tunstall. 'The boats themselves are in very many instances scarcely fit to be used; old and worn out, leaky and therefore very damp, never painted or well cleaned for years (beyond an occasional fumigation), and consequently filthy beyond description,' he wrote of the boats carrying ironstone from Warwickshire and Staffordshire. And over the whole country he claimed 'there are between 80,000 and 100,000 men, women and children, passing through large centres of population, who are the most uncared-for, forgotten, neglected, drunken, ignorant and degraded human beings in this our boasted land of civilisation and such as are not to be met with on the face of the whole earth.'

Although Smith's case for reform was a good one, there is little doubt that he overstated it. Moreover, even if his claims were justified, he directed his attack rather against the morals of

A scene below Buckby Lock on the Grand Junction Canal, photographed in about 1913 (*Waterways Museum*)

the boat people than against the economic system that reduced them to the physical state in which he found them. This system required them to work very long hours out of doors through all extremes of weather with bouts of heavy manual labour and periods of frustrating delays and, for the family boaters, gave them no home other than their workplace, the boat itself, to return to. Their only refuge was the public house, of which there were plenty along the towpath—about six or seven for every one that is open today. For the children, education was virtually impossible, and daily life for the young, hardly any of whom ever learned to swim, was beset by dangers. Only the nonconformist missionaries seemed, in the later years of the nineteenth century, to take much interest in the boat people's welfare, with the Seamen and Boatmen's Friend Society and the Salvation Army doing much good work.

The public image of the boat people in Smith's day was an unfavourable one. An article in the *Birmingham Daily Mail* of March 1875, which Smith himself quoted, describes the boatman as 'to a great extent a social pariah, a water Ishmael'. The writer comments on the usual scenes of canal life, as seen from a country bridge:

> The slow, plodding, ragged old horse, feeding as he goes along from a tin bucket; the long, ugly, deep-laden boat, with its smoky chimney and flashily painted flat-topped cabin; the brawny fellow in the bright plush waistcoat, huge lace-up boots and fur cap, who drives the horse and shambles sulkily along, and the faded woman in rusty, ragged attire, half masculine, half feminine, who steers.

To observers, their dress, as well as their way of life, marked the boat people as different. In a succeeding article the same writer mentions 'the sleeved plush-fronted waistcoats, the thick blanket-coats, and beloved fur caps, and mighty hob-nailed lace-up boots', which were made and sold in the various water-side settlements. Many labourers in the Victorian era, however, would have worn similar clothes and it is doubtful whether away from their boats the canal people would have been easily identifiable. Embroidered belts and braces were popular with some of the men, and women often wore quite elaborate bonnets, but on the whole the style and quality of the clothes reflected the boaters' economic position rather than their trade.

It certainly seems that in the later years of commercial boating, when the canals were very much the poor relation of inland transport, some of the pride in appearance was lost. And at no time in canal history does the element of water seem to have affected the dress of those who worked upon it; aprons for women and jackets for men were the usual apparel as witnessed by photographs taken over the past hundred years.

Society in general, however, came to regard the boat people as a race apart, certainly those who through economic necessity spent their lives and bred their children on the boats. Early in this century romantic accounts of their origins became current and for a time they seemed to be established as 'water gypsies' in the public mind. 'Undoubtedly they are of southern extraction. Their dark, black hair, their olive skin, that soft expression of lethargy in the eyes, all point to the blood of some race other than the fair-haired Saxon,' wrote E. Temple Thurston in *The Flower of Gloster* (1911). Yet the evidence seems to be that they simply stepped off the land and into the boats. Although the great majority of boatmen were employed by the carrying companies and worked for a weekly wage, some families lived on the boats for three generations as owners of their own vessels. It was these owner-boatmen, the 'Number Ones', that the public imagination seized upon and gave an idealised image to. Certainly it would seem that the Number Ones in general took pride in the condition of their craft, in its colourful appearance and in its cleanliness; they valued their independence and worked hard in order to survive. Their numbers, however, were comparatively few; no more than one in ten of all canal boats were worked by their owners, and those mostly on the Oxford and Grand Junction canals. Many of the larger carrying companies had well over a hundred boats in their fleet and there was a considerable number of smaller carriers operating locally. As employers the larger firms had fair reputations; some of the smaller ones, however, depending on cost-cutting to obtain trade, were less admirable. Wages on the whole were rather above average for the labouring population although when the canals were iced up, for instance, wages were either stopped or reduced by half. There were nevertheless plenty of opportunities to add to the larder by a bit of poaching or 'gardening' on the journey, or even, for those who traded to the docks, for

31

smuggling. The cellar bar of The Swan at Fradley Junction is said to have been a popular meeting place for the exchange of smuggled brandy.

Generalisations about the life of the boating people can only be misleading. With the demise of commercial carrying, those who regret its passing have tended to dwell on the more picturesque elements of the boat families' life, while the social reformers and proponents of other forms of transport have concentrated on the difficulties and discomforts. Harry Hanson's book *Canal People* gives a fair coverage of both sides and is valuable reading if you want to know more about the subject and examine some of the evidence for yourself.

As you walk the towpaths, look out for the names of the full-length narrow boats. They range from matter-of-fact place names *(Alton, Nuneaton, Northwich)* to more romantic names *(Vienna* now at Cheddleton Mill on the Caldon Canal), astronomical *(Capella, Satellite, Jupiter),* ferocious *(Jaguar)* and dignified *(President).* Some have long histories and many private owners preserve the names of converted narrow boats, handing the name on to a successor when the original boat succumbs to old age. Narrow-boat names reflect both the working and the picturesque aspects of the canals. You will not find on a narrow boat the jokey or suggestive appellations that owners sometimes give to more frivolous vessels. Look out also on the Grand Union Canal for the most attractive travelling advertisements of all, the Ovaltine boats. They used to carry coal but were painted with the motto 'Drink Delicious Ovaltine for Health' in yellow on brown, an inland echo of the advertising slogans painted on the sails of some Thames spritsail barges. They were revived a few years ago and you may be lucky enough to see them.

Today's walker, however, seldom observes the narrow boats to their best advantage. Almost all of those you do see, whether in their original state or converted for pleasure cruising, ride high in the water. Fully loaded boats seem to swim through the water, their hulls almost totally submerged with only a couple of inches of freeboard showing and with the canvas sidecloths raised, the decorative paintwork just skimming the surface of the canal. A loaded pair coming towards you, especially through the mist of an early morning, is an unforgettable sight.

4

CANALS WITHOUT WATER

There are nearly a hundred abandoned and derelict canals in Britain, many of which have almost disappeared from modern maps. Some have been swallowed up in urban or industrial development or obliterated by the plough but there are many lengths that make fascinating walking. Detailed accounts of a few of the more rewarding walks can be found in Part II. This chapter gives brief references to several more where access is easy and there is plenty to see. Be careful not to trespass on private property and to enquire about right of access if you are not certain.

In the south of England the line of the Wey & Arun Junction Canal is a popular walk. This runs from the River Wey at Shalford, south of Guildford, to the Arun near Billingshurst. The canal, legally abandoned in 1868, is gradually being restored and the Wey & Arun Canal Trust publishes a guide for walkers, *Wey–South Path*. The canal is eighteen and a half miles in length and it is worth doing the whole walk if possible; there are twenty-three locks to trace in a fascinating journey between the North and South Downs. In a more advanced state of restoration is the Basingstoke Canal, much of which is in water. You can follow this throughout its length from the River Wey at West Byfleet to Greywall Tunnel, near North Warnborough. The twelve miles between Woking and Ash Vale are probably the most enjoyable with many locks and a variety of scenery. These two canals are the most convenient for those living in the London area as both Guildford and Woking are readily accessible by train.

From Swindon you can walk much of the line of the Wiltshire & Berkshire Canal, which ran from Abingdon on the Thames to Semington on the Kennet & Avon Canal. Most of this canal is wholly derelict and several lengths are missing from the Ordnance Survey maps. Itineraries are available, however;

contact a public library or the Wiltshire & Berkshire Canal Amenity Group for advice. Although your walk will be through fine country, there are few canal-associated structures to see.

The Wiltshire & Berkshire connected via the North Wiltshire Canal—most of which has disappeared—with the Thames & Severn. This makes a much more rewarding walk and can be followed from its junction with the Stroudwater Canal at Stroud (*see* Part II) to its meeting with the Thames at Inglesham, just above Lechlade. The first stretch from Stroud to Chalford is nothing special, but this is soon over and the rest of the walk is rich with scenic variety as you gradually ascend through the Golden Valley to the great summit tunnel at Sapperton and thence past the source of the Thames, the site of Thames Head Pumping Station, and the villages of Siddington, South Cerney, Cerney Wick, Latton and Cricklade. A towpath guide to the canal, by Michael Handford and David Viner, is now available and will help you understand what once happened on this fascinating canal and what is happening now, as it is currently the subject of an ambitious restoration scheme.

The Somersetshire Coal Canal, which joined the Kennet & Avon some five miles south-east of Bath, makes good walking with even something of a climb at Combe Hay. Further west, Taunton is a convenient centre for three interesting walks. The Bridgwater & Taunton Canal can be followed for its 15¼ miles along the towpath; it is watered and navigable by light craft. Between Creech St Michael on this canal and Chard, a distance of 13½ miles, is the Chard Canal—or rather traces of it. This is not ideal for the walker as parts of the line are inaccessible or obliterated, but at Ilminster and Wrantage there are tunnels, inclined planes and remains of the canal bed.

Westward from Taunton runs the Grand Western Canal. The first part of this is very much for the indefatigable enthusiast; interest mainly lies in the remains of its seven lifts but, without clear indications of what you are looking for, it is easy to miss them. There are itineraries in Helen Harris's book *The Grand Western Canal* and in my *Lost Canals and Waterways of Britain*. The western half of the Grand Western, however, has been recently restored and provides a beautiful 11-mile towpath walk from Lowdwells to Tiverton. Begin and end at Tiverton if you are dependent on public transport.

In west Devon is the Tavistock Canal, providing a pleasant walk of three miles from the site of the wharf, now a car park at the end of Canal Road in Tavistock, to the northern portal of Morwelldown Tunnel. The canal feeds water to a generating station at Morwellham. The southern portal of the tunnel, with the rest of the canal and the track of the inclined plane down which cargoes were transported to the port of Morwellham on the Tamar, is now in the keeping of the Morwellham Open Air Museum which is well worth visiting, recreating as it does the industrial past of this area once famous for its export trade in copper.

Another Westcountry canal that makes excellent walking is the Bude Canal, which runs through green rolling countryside. The Bude Canal mostly overcame gradients by inclined planes which took it up 345ft above the port of Bude. You can walk from Bude, where the lowest length is still in water, and up the two longest inclines at Marhamchurch and Hobbacott Down (seek permission from Thurlibeer Farm for the latter). You may either continue along the main line to Holsworthy, follow the feeder arm to Tamar Lake or, for the longest walk, try to trace the Druxton Branch to Crossgate, three miles from Launceston. As with the Grand Western Canal you will need an itinerary, to be found either in my *Lost Canals and Waterways of Britain* or in greater detail in *The Bude Canal* by Helen Harris and Monica Ellis. With a total length of 35½ miles the Bude Canal makes a splendid expedition for a long weekend.

In the West Midlands the Droitwich Canal, seven miles long from Droitwich to the Severn at Hawford, is being actively restored by the Droitwich Canals Trust, whose members have cleared the towpath throughout and erected signposts. Up-to-date information and a towpath guide may be obtained from the Trust at Lock Cottage, Ladywood, Droitwich WR9 0AJ. This walk gives you the opportunity to study at close quarters the realities of canal restoration. The Trust intends eventually to restore also the short, heavily locked Droitwich Junction Canal which provides a link with the Worcestershire & Birmingham Canal at Hanbury Junction.

Abandoned canals in Shropshire provide two good middle distance walks. The Shrewsbury Canal extends from the outskirts of Shrewsbury to the slope of the inclined plane at Trench on the A518 in Telford, a distance of 17 miles. Some diversions may be necessary but most of the line is identifiable and there are some fascinating remnants of guillotine locks to be found. At Wappenshall the Shrewsbury Canal made a junction with the Newport Branch of the Shropshire Union and you can follow the branch for 10½ miles to its termination at Norbury Junction on the main line. The branch is accessible from Newport if you want a shorter walk; some of it, however, has been filled in.

In the East Midlands there is a variety of canalside walks. The top section of the Cromford Canal is being restored. You can walk the towpath from the basin at Cromford to Ambergate. If you have time and energy to spare, this can be included in a walk along the line of the Cromford and High Peak Railway. Your canal walk takes you across the substantial Wigwell Aqueduct, past Leawood Pump House—you may be lucky enough to find the engine in steam—and through the short Gregory Tunnel. This is a walk of some seven miles, and though you are close to road and railway throughout you are surprisingly unaware of them.

If you find yourself in Worksop try the abandoned section of the Chesterfield Canal which you can follow for six miles to the eastern portal of Norwood Tunnel. This section is in water as it feeds the navigable length below Worksop, though the going may not be easy. There are several locks and the attractive canalside settlement of Turnerwood to see. Apart from one or two short stretches, it is not practicable to walk the canal west of the tunnel as much of it is inaccessible.

The longest East Midlands walk is provided by the Grantham Canal, 33 miles between Grantham and Nottingham. This is a gentle, winding, rural waterway, shown throughout on the map and with a towpath mostly cleared by the Grantham Canal Restoration Society. You pass eighteen locks as you ramble from village to village through fine rolling country, the only menace coming from the National Coal Board's proposal for opencast mining.

Moving northwards, there are three interesting abandoned canals in the Manchester area. There are some traces of the Manchester, Bolton & Bury Canal in Salford, but for a continuous walk find the canal at Ringley, near Kearsley, and follow it north-westward. Soon you will cross the Prestolee Aqueduct over the Irwell; then you arrive at a basin and can continue up the slope, formed by the remains of a flight of six locks, and along the towpath for nearly five miles to Bury. Apart from a short section, the Bolton arm has been obliterated.

A far longer walk is provided by the Rochdale Canal. You can get to it in the centre of Manchester at Castlefield, Princess Street or Dale Street, where the waterway is navigable. It does not remain navigable for long; see what you think of the treatment of the canal as you approach and walk through the Rochdale Canal Park. You climb through Rochdale, where the canal has been treated rather differently, and reach the summit level north of Littleborough. Here you can best appreciate the achievement of the builders of this canal, and the efforts of the early boatmen who used it. Soon the descent begins, through Todmorden and down the Calder Valley, with an aqueduct over the Calder at Hebden Bridge. The canal terminates at Sowerby Bridge where it makes a junction with the Calder & Hebble Canal. The total length is 33 miles, during which you pass 92 locks with stonework and engineering as fine as any in the country.

Manchester is also the terminus of the Huddersfield Narrow Canal, built with narrow locks to provide an alternative route across the Pennines and to link the Ashton Canal with Sir John Ramsden's Broad Canal in Huddersfield. This is 20 miles long and walkable throughout, and a really splendid walk it is, crowned by a diversion over the top of Standedge Tunnel, the longest canal tunnel in the country. The Huddersfield Canal Society publishes a profusely illustrated and very detailed guide for the towpath walker, obtainable from the Secretary at 28 Cinderhills Road, Holmfirth.

In Yorkshire there is a bracing 9½-mile walk alongside the Pocklington Canal, which is gradually being restored to navigation. The canal is notable for its especially fine road overbridges. This is a walk of changing landscape: placid, gentle hills near Pocklington and the wetlands known as the 'ings' as you approach the Derwent. Wheldrake Ings is a nature reserve and this walk is a treat for ornithologists.

On the other side of the country, the towpath of the 15-mile abandoned northern section of the Lancaster Canal is a public right of way from the southern edge of Kendal to the flight of eight derelict locks at Tewitfield where road construction truncated the waterway, although the Kendal–Stainton length was closed and drained in 1955. This is a most attractive walk, much of it through fields close to the River Kent, with several substantial aqueducts and about fifty-four bridges. There is no towpath through Hincaster Tunnel but you can follow the horse-path across the top. From Stainton southwards the channel is watered and there are proposals for limited restoration of this stretch.

Apart from the Llangollen and the Brecon & Abergavenny, none of the Welsh canals is navigable. The Montgomeryshire is under gradual restoration (*see* Part II) and the Tennant, privately owned and not accessible without permission, is used as a water supply channel; otherwise, all have been abandoned. The Monmouthshire Canal can be walked from its junction with the Brecon & Abergavenny to the outskirts of Newport; it is in water and some of it is in good order. You can also follow most of its Crumlin Branch from the M4 crossing, through attractive Allt-y-ryn, up the fourteen Rogerstone locks and on to Cwmcarn. In the next valley to the west the Glamorganshire Canal provides a nine-mile walk from Merthyr to Abercynon,

Bow-hauling on the Edinburgh & Glasgow Union Canal to the east of Avon Aqueduct, 1951 *(Railway & Canal Historical Society; M. Wheeler)*

although south of here much has been obliterated by road building. Further west still the Neath Canal runs close to the A465 from Glyn-neath to Aberdulais; you will see evidence of preservation work in the locks, and an industrial history park is planned for Resolven. Last of the major valley canals, the Swansea, is close to the A4067 and can be followed from Abercrave to Clydach; again, most of the lower section has been obliterated. Of these South Wales canals, the Monmouthshire and the Neath provide most interest for the walker.

The two great lowland Scottish canals, the Forth & Clyde and the Edinburgh & Glasgow Union, were both abandoned in the early 1960s. Boats can still use some stretches but culverting, infilling and other obstructions prevent through navigation. It is, however, possible to walk the length of both with only a few diversions. Glasgow to Edinburgh by towpath would make a walk of rather over fifty miles, via Kirkintilloch, Falkirk (where the canals once met by The Union Inn, although the flight of locks that made the connection has now been obliterated), Linlithgow, Broxburn and Ratho. There are splendid aqueducts, Kelvin on the Forth & Clyde and Avon, Almond and Slateford on the Union, fine canalside buildings at Port Dundas in Glasgow and in the towns through which the canals pass, impressive flights of locks at Maryhill in Glasgow and at Falkirk, a tunnel at Falkirk on the Union, a canal museum at Linlithgow and a restaurant boat, *Pride of the Union*, on the approach to Edinburgh. There are no problems of access and both canals are shown fully on the Ordnance Survey maps. West of Glasgow you can walk out to Bowling Basin on the Clyde, terminus of the Forth & Clyde. The basins in Edinburgh, however, have been filled in and the ABC cinema in Lothian Road now stands on the site of Port Hopetoun.

5
NATURAL HISTORY

Anyone who visits canals frequently soon becomes aware of the necessity—and difficulty—of preserving and maintaining the environmental balance essential if the natural life of the waterway and the towpath is to flourish. For the most part, as the presence of anglers indicates, canals are clean enough to support a good measure of underwater life; the bad old days of extreme pollution when blue flames played over the surface of the Bradford Canal are thankfully gone. From time to time toxic elements do find their way into canals; heavy rainstorms may bring weedkiller or other agricultural chemicals into the channel or canalside industry may contaminate the water with its effluent. Contrary to what some anglers maintain, boats cause little pollution and that only from accidental spillage of fuel. Patches of oil in the water are more likely to come from nearby garages or factories than from boats.

The presence of boats, however, does affect the natural life of the canal. A rural waterway which is abandoned and neglected becomes filled in as reeds gradually take over, extinguishing other vegetation and filling up the channel. Canalside trees become overgrown and alders grow quickly, cutting off sunlight needed for the survival of other plants. Movement of water may cease altogether and slowly the canal dies. Restoration involves clearing and dredging the channel, cutting back, removing or trimming the trees, clearing the towpath and laying the towpath hedge. Plants begin to grow again, fish and small animals reappear; the water comes to life. Back come the boats—for this is the purpose of the restoration exercise—and, provided that there are not too many of them and they observe the 4mph speed limit, all should be well. Too many boats, travelling or trying to travel too fast, will prove destructive. The wash wears away the banks and destroys the plants on the waterline and the rapidly churning propellors keep the mud sediment in suspension preventing light from reaching underwater plants. The towpath walker is in the best position to appreciate this and, if he has the necessary botanical knowledge, will find it interesting to keep a record of what he observes.

In many areas canals, artificial in origin though they are, provide some of the few surviving wetland sites. Much of the old wetland has disappeared with improved drainage for the extension of ploughland and building. Swans, moorhens, coots and mallards find refuge on canals, as do such spectacular birds as the heron and kingfisher. Frogs and toads, water voles and water shrews are all common, and at night foxes may come to drink. On a recently surveyed stretch of the Trent & Mersey Canal to the east of Stafford, between Colton and Wolseley Bridge, there are masses of typical vegetation, such as sweet grass, great hairy willow herb and meadowsweet, woody nightshade, marsh woundwort and skullcap. Here and there are clumps of less common wetland plants including brooklime, celery-leaved crowfoot and gipsywort. In the reed-swamp vegetation beyond Wolseley Bridge you find bur-reed and pond sedge with freshwater mussels on the canal bed. Among the birds noted, as well as herons and kingfishers, are warblers, siskins and finches.

In the countryside, canals are unique in providing within only a few yards several different habitats. Of great importance is the hedge by the towpath, its age established by the date when the canal was cut, and sometimes the only surviving hedge of any length in the immediate area. It provides a home for nesting birds and small animals. Along the towpath itself you can often find a whole variety of plants and the butterflies and insects attracted by them. By the water's edge grow marsh plants and different varieties of reeds. The canal supports floating-leaved plants, such as water lilies; many more plants live entirely submerged.

The canal can also be seen as a corridor linking fields, marshes and woodlands, encouraging plants and animals to spread. The yellow monkey flower, introduced into Britain in 1812, and Canadian pondweed, imported at the end of the nineteenth century, have both spread throughout the countryside via the canal network, and the floating water-plantain, generally found only in the west, has moved along the

Ellel Grange Bridge on the Lancaster Canal *(British Waterways Board)*

Montgomeryshire Canal into Shropshire. Birds and small mammals make use of the comparative security of the corridor which also attracts a wide variety of insect life, especially butterflies and dragonflies.

Of the navigable canals, the Brecon & Abergavenny must rank among the most interesting for the variety of wildlife—plant, bird and animal—to be found along its course. The Southern Oxford Canal and the Leicester arm of the Grand Union are also especially rich in wildlife, with the Shropshire Union, Staffordshire & Worcestershire and Worcester & Birmingham as close rivals. On some unnavigable stretches of canals nature reserves have been established, for example on the Cromford Canal between Whatstandwell and Ambergate. There is a canal bank nature trail between Field End Bridge and Stainton on the abandoned northern length of the Lancaster Canal, cared for by the Cumbria Trust for Nature Conservation and providing for the county 'a unique habitat of near-stagnant

42

water, wooded banks, scrub, reeds and open fields beyond'. Among other canal nature trails is one at Tring reservoirs, adjacent to the Grand Union main line; the Widcombe and Bath Nature Trail incorporating much of the towpath of the Kennet & Avon in that area; the Market Drayton Nature Trail, which includes stretches of the Shropshire Union; the Almond Valley Nature Trail by the Almond Aqueduct of the Edinburgh & Glasgow Union Canal; the Hay Head Nature Trail alongside the Daw End Branch of the Birmingham Canal Navigations; and the Prees Branch Nature Reserve at the end of the old Prees Branch of the Shropshire Union Canal. A particularly novel trail begins at Loughborough and follows the towpath of the Grand Union and River Soar, branching off through Quorndon Park to the village of Quorn. From the station here you can return to Loughborough by steam train (on most weekends anyway) operated by the Main Line Steam Trust. A British Waterways Board information sheet, entitled 'A Walk on the Wildside', gives you a list of addresses from which you can obtain guides to all or most of these trails.

The Leeds & Liverpool Canal has been described as 'a linear nature reserve' but the description is applicable to the great majority of canals except where pollution, insensitive landscaping or serious vandalism have occurred. At the time of their construction, and for some years afterwards, canals were raw gashes across the countryside and their promoters were attacked as despoilers of natural beauty. They have, as the canalscape has matured, become natural havens; restrictions of access and lack of opportunities for development have kept the more modern despoilers away. It is remarkable how attitudes have changed in the past few years. Tactful adaptation of old buildings and the harmonious design of new ones now characterise many boatyards; the Yorkshire Dales boatyard at Banknewton on the Leeds & Liverpool Canal and Robin Tod's yard on the Brecon & Abergavenny Canal at Llanfoist are exceptionally beautiful in their settings.

6

PREPARING TO WALK

Equipment for towpath walking is comparatively simple. Most important is a good pair of boots; proper walking boots, as waterproof as possible, are best. In more remote areas towpaths are sometimes eroded or waterlogged and they are often muddy. Otherwise wear whatever is comfortable while remembering the hazards of brambles and stinging nettles.

You are not likely to need a compass, except when trying to trace the courses of the most derelict canals, but a good map will add much to the enjoyment and understanding of your walk. The Ordnance Survey 1: 50,000 (Landranger) sheets are usually adequate, though if you can afford them the 1: 25,000 may be more helpful. In urban areas a locally published A to Z guide is useful, especially for finding access points.

The cruising guides are of comparatively little use to the walker except for indicating the proximity of pubs and shops. The new Nicholson's guides are fairly helpful; better are those published by the monthly magazine *Waterways World*, although these cover only the more popular cruising navigations: the Shropshire Union, Oxford, Staffordshire & Worcestershire, Llangollen and Trent & Mersey canals.

Most useful are the towpath guides. These can be obtained from canal shops, by post from the Inland Waterways Association or *Waterways World* book service or possibly from local bookshops. Those currently available include Langford's *The Staffordshire & Worcestershire Canal*, Stevens' *The Brecknock & Abergavenny and Monmouthshire Canals,* Clew's *Wessex Waterway*, the Huddersfield Canal Society's *The Huddersfield Canals Towpath Guide,* Chester-Brown's *The Other Sixty Miles* (abandoned canals of Birmingham), Pratt's *Discovering London's Canals,* Biddle's *Lancashire Waterways*, Smith's *Yorkshire Waterways,* Owen's *Cheshire Waterways*, the London Tourist Board's *London's Canal Walks* and my own *Dis-*

44

covering Lost Canals. Full details of all these books are given in the Bibliography.

Leaflets, booklets and pamphlets dealing with individual canals may also be available, often issued by the respective canal society. These are not necessarily always kept in print; if you are planning in advance a walk along a particular canal, it is worth enquiring from the local reference library whether a guide exists, or contacting the secretary of the local canal society—again, the reference library should be able to provide an address.

Planning in advance adds greatly to the interest of a walk. For a knowledge of the history and development of the canal system, the most comprehensive and accurate study is Charles Hadfield's *British Canals,* now in its seventh edition. Canals in the various regions are examined in greater detail in the series 'Canals of the British Isles' published by David & Charles. Full histories of individual canals, some of which contain detailed itineraries, have also been written, although many of them are out of print and available only secondhand or from libraries.

A canalside pub at Gnossal on the Shropshire Union *(British Waterways Board)*

Details of a number of these are given in the Bibliography; many of them are published by David & Charles in their 'Inland Waterways Histories' series.

Other books which should prove of interest include Gagg's *Observer's Book of Canals*, McKnight's *The Shell Book of Inland Waterways*, Paget-Tomlinson's *The Complete Book of Canal and River Navigations*, and Rolt's *The Inland Waterways of England* and *Navigable Waterways*. Of course, Rolt's classic *Narrow Boat*, first published in 1944, is still unequalled as a personal testimony to the beauty and appeal of our canals. A bookseller who specialises in waterways books is M. Baldwin of 98 Kenyon Street, London SW6 6LB (telephone 01–385 2036). The monthly magazines *Waterways World* and *Canal and Riverboat* sometimes contain articles of interest to the towpath walker, and advice may also be obtained from your local branch of the Inland Waterways Association, membership of which can be of value both to you and to the cause of canal restoration and retention.

Summer is the least satisfactory season of the year for towpath walking. Canalside vegetation tends to grow with extra luxuriance and the aggressive greenery conceals objects of interest such as mileposts and boundary markers. The smaller canalside buildings may be completely obscured and the surrounding countryside screened from view. The towpath itself is often crowded with local strollers and surplus boat crews, and the sound of the transistor radio may be heard on the land. Tracing abandoned canals is especially difficult in summer when their channels become completely overgrown. Late autumn, winter and spring are ideal and a touch of frost in the air stimulates the breathing and encourages the limbs. If boats attract you, the disadvantage will be that you will see fewer of them, especially as the idea of a 'cruising season' from Easter to September seems to have taken hold of the authorities and much of the boating public in recent years. But the pubs will be less busy and the lock-keepers and lengthsmen you may meet will have more time to chat. It is surprising what you can learn from those who live and work, or have worked, alongside the canal. But do remember to respect the privacy of those who live in boats or canalside cottages and resist the temptation to peer into windows or take short cuts through canalside gardens.

If possible, make a note or take a photograph of anything interesting you see for which there does not seem to be a clear or obvious explanation. Later, try to discover that explanation, either from the nearest British Waterways Board office, a local historian, the secretary of the local canal society (if one exists) or by writing to the correspondence columns of a waterway magazine or to the Railway and Canal Historical Society, whose membership includes most of the leading canal historians and experts. Your question may inspire some researcher and lead to a real discovery; there are plenty of discoveries still to be made about the history and working practices of the various canals.

Camera, binoculars, notebook, wild flower or bird guide—I have not dealt with these as all or some of them are part of the normal equipment of the serious walker. What gives towpath walking its special attraction is the fascination of the water with its changing reflections and perspectives, stretching and curving before you, leading you on past structures of wood and stone, brick and iron, created by man to suit his own scale and his own speed, the labour of the past for the delight of the present. It costs you nothing and it is there for you to enjoy.

Part II
THE WALKS

7 THE BOW BACK RIVERS OF EAST LONDON · Philip Daniell *(3 miles)*

This walk takes you to some forgotten waterways of East London which few people explore. The starting point is Bromley-by-Bow Underground Station (London Transport District and Metropolitan Lines) which is adjacent to the A102 (M). Cars can park in the streets behind the station.

From the station, cross the road by the pedestrian tunnel and then, a few yards north, follow Three Mills Lane to cross the River Lee Navigation. Now on either side of you are two of the finest old waterside buildings in London, both of them tide mills. On the left is the House Mill, with four undershot waterwheels. Built in 1776 and now a Grade I Listed Building, it is to become an industrial museum. On the right are the Clock Mill and oast houses. This three-wheeled mill was built in 1817, but the octagonal clock tower is older. A short diversion south along the Lee takes you to Bow Locks beyond which the navigation becomes tidal. At the right state of the tide, you may see a tug drawing a train of lighters, for this is an active commercial waterway.

Beyond the Clock Mill, take a narrow passage to the right. Note the marker indicating high tides of the past. Looking back, you get a fine view of the Mill, and its old cast-iron crane. You walk high above Abbey Creek and soon cross the Prescott Sluice, built as part of a big flood-relief scheme in the early 1930s. Follow the path by extensive reedbeds which line the Channelsea River and then mount steps onto the Northern Outfall Sewer. The magnificent Abbey Mills Pumping Station on the left was built in the 1860s and had eight beam engines to pump water into the sewer.

Walk west along the sewer and turn left along the busy Stratford High Street to a pedestrian underpass. A diversion through it is rewarding. Continue along the High Street on the opposite side and soon turn right along Blaker Road. On the right is a pair of floodgates, and on the left the derelict Marshgate Lock and its lock-house. Several boats have their moorings along the City Mills River here. Return through the underpass

50

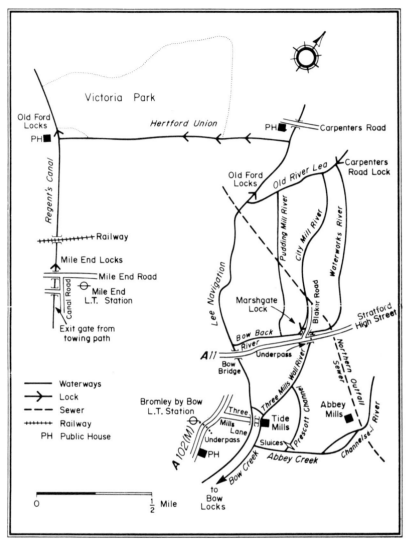

Map 1 The Bow Back Rivers of East London

and, opposite, follow the path high beside the Three Mills Wall River, soon getting a good view of the rear of the House Mill. Recross the Lee, and follow its towing path north. Its good condition is due to the installation of high-voltage electric cables beneath it. You have to leave the path to cross the busy A11, at

51

Bow Bridge. The path is then on the other side of the navigation. Where it passes under the outfall sewer, you can climb onto it and view the surrounding scene.

A new footbridge carries the towing path across the old River Lee. Before crossing it, stroll along the river bank. The structure on the left is what remains of old floodgates. A footbridge takes you over the Pudding Mill River and another (with unusual drainage channels) over the City Mills River, and thus to Carpenters Lock with its uncommon radial gates. Once this area was alive with industry. Now it is occupied only by birds and an astonishing range of plants. On your return, look along the Pudding Mill River and you will see a boat. How it got there or how it will ever get out again, nobody seems to know.

Back at the Lee, cross the footbridge and go on past the mechanised Old Ford Locks. Opposite new landscaped industrial buildings you will see the start of the Hertford Union Canal. To reach it, continue to Carpenters Road, and return by the opposite bank after crossing the bridge. The Hertford Union enables boats to come down from the Regent's Canal to join the

The Clock Mill and oast houses on the Lee Navigation, part of the Three Mills Conservation Area (British Waterways Board)

Lee by three locks. The towing path runs beside Victoria Park;
by turning right when you join the Regent's Canal you can soon
enter the park at another Old Ford Locks. Opposite is The
Royal Cricketers, a pub with a canalside terrace, and The RIs
Afloat, a licensed restaurant. (Cars can be parked in Victoria
Park, near the canal, so this is an alternative starting point for
the walk.)

To complete the walk, follow the canal south. The long
canopy of the paper warehouse of Suttons International is a
reminder that the canal was once an artery of commerce. After
passing under a railway bridge, and a fine terrace of new canalside houses on the offside, go through a black gate to cross a
grassed area and follow Canal Road beside the waterway. Walk
east along Mile End Road to Mile End Underground Station
and take a train to Bromley-by-Bow.

The Regent's Canal provides a complete contrast to the
sequestered route of the first part of the walk. Along the
Regent's Canal, the Canal Way Parks are being created by the
Greater London Council in co-operation with borough councils
and the British Waterways Board. The canal towing path, much
improved by landscaping and the provision of information
boards, is a link between open spaces, present and potential.
The evidence is visible on the last stretch of the walk.

On the Back Rivers, since there are no customers, there are
no pubs. A little beyond Carpenters Road Bridge is The Lea
Tavern. Snacks are available at The Royal Cricketers, opposite
Victoria Park. There are several pubs near Bromley-by-Bow
Station. My favourite is The Queen Victoria in Gillinder
Street, south on the east side of the A102(M). It is a free house,
and has some interesting bygones in its bar.

To go south from Bromley-by-Bow station by car, you
should head north on the dual carriageway as far as the A11
roundabout. Coming south by car, you will pass the station and
soon take a road to the left to pass under the dual carriageway
and then head north again. Despite numerous visits to this area,
I find the roads as confusing as, at first, were the nine channels
of the Bow Back Rivers.

The towing paths on the first part of the walk may be under
water at high tide in the Thames. Local radio stations usually
announce the time of high tide, or ask your public library.

8 THE BRECON & ABERGAVENNY CANAL · Adrian Russell

Cwm Crawnon to Talybont (4 or 9 miles)

The Brecon & Abergavenny Canal is situated wholly within the Brecon Beacons National Park and traverses outstandingly beautiful countryside for almost all of its course. The whole towpath is well worth walking. If your time is limited, however, the section from Cwm Crawnon to Talybont is recommended, with both terminals on the Abergavenny to Brecon bus route, service 42. Alternatively, you can make it into a round trip by returning from Talybont around the Tor-y-foel mountain, giving a total length of 9 miles.

The canal was opened in 1800, making an end-on junction with the Monmouthshire Canal at Pontymoile. The combined waterways carried coal and iron down to Newport; the Brecon & Abergavenny passed through rich farmland as well, supplying lime and manure and distributing farm produce. It is the canal featured in Alexander Cordell's well-known novel *Rape of the Fair Country*. It traded successfully until the 1850s when the tramroads that served it were bought by railway companies and traffic began to decline. Many of the ironworks were closed when the Bessemer and open hearth methods were adopted, although a little commercial traffic did continue until 1933 and for a further five years on the Monmouthshire. In recent years much restoration work has been undertaken and it remains open to boats for all of its length, incorporating the first mile of the Monmouthshire until the culverted Crown Bridge at Sebastopol.

Cwm Crawnon is about a mile from the small village of Llangynidr. The walk starts near the Coach and Horses, a popular pub serving a wide range of excellent bar food. Access to the towpath is on the far side of the road bridge above Llangynidr Bottom Lock. From the lock, face the recently reconstructed bridge and begin walking, noting a broken milestone indicating that Pontymoile is 23 miles behind you. The Newport Waterworks pipeline, bringing water from the Talybont reservoir, crosses the canal here.

Around the corner is a wealth of fascination. The main structure is the aqueduct over the Crawnon, both arches of which you can descend to examine. Back on the towpath look for a windlass operated by marlin spikes to open a wooden plug in the canal bed to drain the canal for maintenance. The water exits through a clay pipe on the side of the aqueduct. Notice also the grooves for stop planks, used in conjunction with the drainage plug. A feeder leat from the Crawnon higher up its valley enters the canal here; you can follow this and find a culvert with a measuring device known as a Munro which calculates the volume of water passing according to its height, thus enabling water charges to be established. The valley falls quite dramatically here and you can see potholes in the sandstone blocks, examples of river erosion.

Lock 65 is a few yards further on; in fact, there are only six locks on this canal and the numbering includes those on the Monmouthshire, starting from Newport. The lock falls 10½ft and there is another Munro on the bypass channel. The small

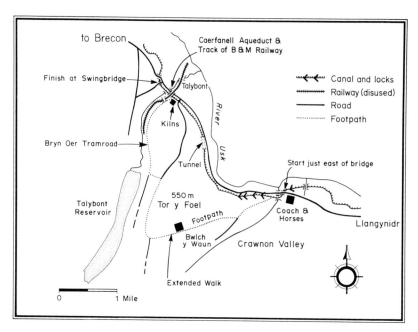

Map 2 The Brecon & Abergavenny Canal: Cwm Crawnon to Talybont

building on the wharf above the lock is the old toll-house where the last toll was collected in 1933. The canal building above it is a maintenance shed, with a single lime kiln behind it. If you have time, visit Robbie at the lock-house on the road below. He runs his own information centre and is a fount of knowledge about the canal; he will give the genuine enthusiast a warm welcome.

A short pound of no more than a hundred yards leads to Lock 66, with the next two locks following so closely that side ponds were constructed to take off the discharged water. Lock 68 is the top of the flight of five which has a total fall of 48ft and stretches for half a mile. The towpath has been recently improved in the area. With the surrounding woodland and hills and the atmosphere of peaceful remoteness, this has been described as the most beautiful setting for locks anywhere. The half-mile post denotes 32½ miles from Newport or 23½ miles from Pontymoile.

As you continue, note the boundary posts of the Great Western Railway which owned the canal in its later years of trading. Diamond-shaped signs still survive on some bridges, denoting their carrying capacity. Bridge 136 is called Workhouse Bridge; the whitewashed stone cottages close by once formed a workhouse, and the ducks in the canal are tame.

The next two and a half miles or so make a superb country walk following the contours of the Usk valley, although the towpath is not in the best condition, being muddy and uneven. The banks are mostly tree-lined; the minor road, close by, is generally very quiet. Among the birds you may see are wheatears, whinchats, buzzards, merlin, red grouse, dippers, kingfishers and herons.

Various feeder streams flow into the canal, and near the small church of St Detyws you will see another drain plug lacking its windlass. The substantial farmhouse on your right is Llandetty Hall, and looking right you should see a metal footbridge over the Usk in the grounds of Crosfield House which blends beautifully into its surroundings. After Bridge 141 you approach Ashford Tunnel, the only one on the Brecon & Abergavenny. It is only 375yd long and has very shallow cover; indeed, the little

Walkers on the Brecon & Abergavenny Canal *(British Waterways Board)*

hill could have been pierced by a cutting. If you look through you will note a slight distortion owing to a bend. Below the water level the bed is said to have been raised at the sides to enable the boats to be pushed or poled through rather than legged, as was usual. There is one airshaft and the towpath goes over the top along the minor road itself.

A number of dogs may come to meet you as you arrive at Talybont, well known for its hunt. Car scrapyards are evident and a couple of petrol pumps which date back to the days when petrol was a few shillings a gallon. The old stable and warehouse building on your right has been converted to a private house. The Travellers Rest was a canalside hostelry where boatmen took refreshment. Bridge 142 is a wooden replacement and there is evidence to suggest that it is on the line of a Roman spur road that connected to a Roman road from Caerleon to Brecon. Beyond is Talybont Wharf with a winding point. You can find a row of lime kilns; the Bryn Oer Tramroad, which you may follow later, terminated in front of the kilns. Just past a water pipeline the abandoned Brecon & Merthyr Railway crossed the canal; this took traffic from the canal and accelerated its downfall. The canal is embanked over the village and you look down on the backs of houses including two pubs, The Star and The White Hart—note the horse tether rings on the latter. Between the pubs is a wide stone aqueduct over the River Caerfanell; a run-off leat from the canal drains into the river, via a conventional sluice. In the village you will see a row of surprisingly narrow brick cottages inscribed with the name E. Jenkins, and an old mill once operated by the stream which flows under both the canal and the road. At the end of the village is an electrically operated lifting bridge constructed in 1970; its predecessor had been fixed down and prevented boats from reaching Brecon for many years.

You can either walk on a further 9 miles to Brecon, taking in the pretty village of Pencelli, the Brynich Aqueduct over the Usk and the one remaining lock, or catch a bus at Talybont for Brecon or Abergavenny. Alternatively, you can return to your starting point by another route which will add further variety and interest to your walk.

Return to Bridge 143 and take the line of the Bryn Oer Tramroad, leading you up the Caerfanell valley. The tramroad build-

The White Hart Inn at Talybont on the Brecon & Abergavenny; the entrance to the sluice by the aqueduct can be seen in the left foreground *(A. J. Russell)*

ings have been demolished and the only substantial remains are some stone blocks on which the rails were laid. Most of the rails have been taken by farmers or souvenir hunters. When you reach the height of the Talybont reservoir you will see some ruined buildings and a footpath crossing your track. Follow left alongside a wood which brings you to an unclassified road. Now turn right and follow the road around the summit of the Tor-y-foel mountain. Look for a track to the left, which will take you down to Bwlch-y-wain Farm. There is a right of way through the farmyard and you head on gently descending along the U-shaped Crawnon valley. At the road at the bottom turn left and walk on to Cwm Crawnon.

Other stretches of this canal are equally fascinating with a blend of scenic countryside and industrial archaeology and, if you have the opportunity, you should certainly explore further.

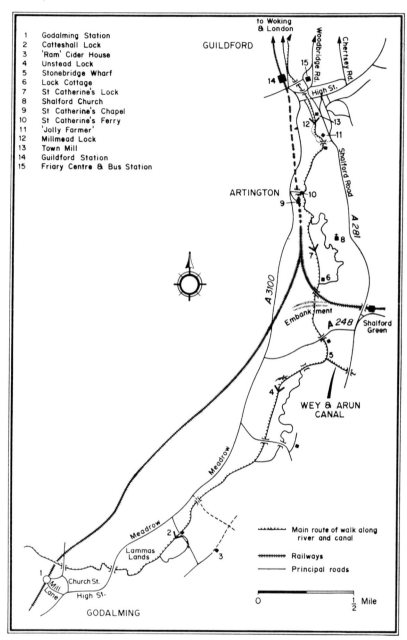

1   Godalming Station
2   Catteshall Lock
3   'Ram' Cider House
4   Unstead Lock
5   Stonebridge Wharf
6   Lock Cottage
7   St Catherine's Lock
8   Shalford Church
9   St Catherine's Chapel
10 St Catherine's Ferry
11 'Jolly Farmer'
12 Millmead Lock
13 Town Mill
14 Guildford Station
15 Friary Centre & Bus Station

GUILDFORD

to Woking
& London

Woodbridge Rd.

Chertsey Rd.

High St.

Shalford Road

A 281

ARTINGTON

A 3100

Embankment

A 248

Shalford
Green

WEY & ARUN
CANAL

Meadrow

Meadrow

Lammas
Lands

Mill
Lane

Church St.

High St.

GODALMING

········ Main route of walk along
          river and canal

┼┼┼┼┼┼┼ Railways

———— Principal roads

0   ½ Mile

Map 3 The Godalming Navigation

60

9 THE GOLDALMING
NAVIGATION · Colin Perris *(4½ miles)*

The Godalming Navigation is a continuation of the Wey Navigation from the Thames at Weybridge to Guildford. It was completed in 1764 and was administered by its own commissioners until it was given in 1968 to the National Trust, who had become the owners of the Wey Navigation five years earlier. Commercial carrying above Guildford had ceased by 1950 but the river has become increasingly popular with pleasure traffic, with narrow boats for hire as well as light craft of all kinds and plenty of moorings for private owners.

From Godalming Station, take the left-hand exit down Station Approach into Borough Road and turn left to Boarden Bridge, a low brick structure over two hundred years old and one of the oldest surviving bridges over the Wey. Take the path just before the road bridge which leads into an attractive cloister with a small garden and fishpond, built in memory of J. G. Phillips, the heroic chief radio operator on the *Titanic*. The nearby church has a fourteenth-century spire. The path follows the windings of the willow-lined river around public gardens and a bowling green to Town Bridge, where you cross the A3100 to regain the footpath on the opposite bank. This bridge is effectively the limit of navigation, twenty miles from the Thames at Weybridge. The river bends right and then sharply left at Godalming Wharf, the most southerly point on the connected inland waterways system in Britain.

Soon you reach a canalised section, the towpath bringing you to Catteshall Lock while the river branches off to the right. Cross the road at Catteshall Bridge, taking care with the heavy towpath gates. Soon you are opposite Farncombe Boathouse, home of Godalming Narrow Boats. The river winds on towards Trowers Bridge, a distinctive old structure with brick side-arches and a flat centre span. You pass carefully tended gardens of pleasant houses and then enter open meadow land, a good area for a picnic with views towards wooded hills. A straight canalised length leads beneath Unstead Bridge; you have to cross the road here and it is worth walking along the road to the right to see the original Unstead Bridge, with its five low arches, now much overgrown and crossing no more than a wide ditch, once the course of the river. Unstead Farm nearby is an attractive timbered Elizabethan building. The reed-lined stretch brings you to Unstead Lock, bordered by light industrial units; this site was an emergency food depot in World War II with supplies being transported mainly by water. The path then continues through a tree-lined stretch, with glimpses of meadows to the right, and crosses a wooden footbridge over an inlet now providing a quiet backwater for a private house. Shortly you pass between the abutments of a demolished railway bridge which once carried the single-track branch line from Guildford to Horsham.

After crossing open pasture, you come to a bend in the river and the entrance to the Wey and Arun Junction Canal, opened in 1816 and closed in 1871 but now being gradually restored by the Wey & Arun Canal Trust. The watered section you can see, however, is only about 250yd long and is used for private moorings. Moorings also line the river past the site of Stonebridge Wharf. The old barn-like building behind a grassy slipway at the end of the moorings was once used for the storage of gunpowder made at the nearby Chilworth factory and taken by boat to the arsenals on the lower Thames. Old canal cottages overlook the wharf. Past the Vulcanised Fibre Works, whose wharf is now disused, is Broadford Bridge, lowest on the navigation with a headroom of only 6ft.

Having crossed the main road, continue along the west bank past an embankment intended to carry a spur line linking the Tonbridge railway to the London–Portsmouth line but never built and beneath a steel girder bridge carrying the Reading–Tonbridge line. Attractive views now open out towards St Catherine's Chapel and the Downs around Guildford. The main river falls away to the right over a weir while the navigation continues in a straight line to St Catherine's Lock. This is a beautiful spot and you may well feel like exploring the area in more detail. The lock-cottage is in a specially delightful setting.

From St Catherine's Lock the towpath continues on the west bank with the main railway line to the left. You enter a pleasantly wooded stretch and the main river rejoins on the right as the railway disappears into a tunnel. Note a vertical roller at a sharp horseshoe bend, left from the days of horse-drawn barges. After the next bend, the towpath, almost obliterated here, rounds the foot of a steep sandy hill on top of which is the ruin of St Catherine's Chapel, though you cannot see it from this point. Immediately beyond is St Catherine's ferry, with water from a spring bubbling down alongside a steep lane that passes Ferry Cottage. The ferry, which ceased operating in 1964, provided a crossing on the line of the old Pilgrim's Way from Winchester to Canterbury. The spring, known locally as Chaucer's Spring, is epitomised by a rhyme on a nearby notice board:

> My downward flow, your upward path,
> Are fixed by law divine;
> My task is to refresh your soul,
> Yours to discover mine.

You may divert up Ferry Lane to the village of Artington on the main Portsmouth road and to climb the hill on which stands St Catherine's Chapel. The lane passes the attractive Pilgrim Cottage and takes you across the railway line between Sand Tunnel and Chalk Tunnel, each named after the soil it penetrates. From the top of the lane a track turns back left up the slope to the hilltop and the ruined chapel, which dates from the early fourteenth century and was a resting place for pilgrims on their way to Canterbury.

Return down the lane to the towpath and walk on past water-meadows backed by Chantries Hill. The navigation passes Guildford Rowing Club on the site of George Davis's Wharf, once a loading point for locally quarried chalk. Note another towline roller as the navigation bends left; next comes Quarry Hill footbridge that leads you off the towpath to the A281 at the southern approach to Guildford and to The Jolly Farmer (not accessible from the towpath). Further along is Guildford Boat-house, with boats for hire and a restaurant boat, the *Alfred Leroy*. You may see canoeists on a slalom course to the left of the weir. To the right a stretch of water, once a millstream, leads to the old Town Mill. Ahead is the popular Millmead Lock, usually crowded with sightseers.

To explore Guildford, cross the footbridge at the lock and take the path alongside the Yvonne Arnaud Theatre, which uses the Town Mill, dating from 1770, as a scenery store and workshop. You can enjoy a circular tour by crossing the main road, Millbrook, and following Rosemary Alley, Quarry Street, turning into Castle Arch, walking round the keep of Guildford Castle, turning right into Castle Street, then left into Tunsgate and on to the High Street climbing up the hill from the river. Though to some extent disfigured by recent buildings, Guildford's High Street is full of architectural interest and it is worth walking as far as the Royal Grammar School, founded in 1507. Return down the hill past the Guildhall and The Angel, an old coaching inn. Turn into Quarry Street by The Star Inn then bear right into Mill Lane which leads to the pedestrian crossing of Millbrook and back to Millmead Lock. Cross the river into Millmead and continue along the waterside opposite the end of the Mill Pool. Walk on to the site of the recently demolished Town Bridge and, just beyond, the site of Town Wharf, the dividing point between the Wey and Godalming Navigations. Nearby is a preserved eighteenth-century wooden treadmill crane, about the only evidence of the trading past of the river.

10 THE HEREFORD & GLOUCESTER CANAL · David Bick

Newent to Dymock (4 miles)

There is no English canal more rural than the Hereford & Gloucester. General trade and the vision of an important coalfield prompted its promotion, but unhappily the local collieries never prospered and in 1798, on reaching from Gloucester to the halfway mark at Ledbury, money ran out and the venture languished for forty years.

Thanks to the determination of a new manager, Stephen Ballard, Hereford was reached at last in 1845, but not until the Canal Age had gone into decline. Half a century later the canal was abandoned when the Great Western Railway converted the Gloucester–Ledbury section into a railway. However, several miles near Newent escaped destruction, including the notorious Oxenhall Tunnel, and can still be explored. This remains one of the most interesting lengths on the whole 34 miles of original waterway, much of which has now disappeared.

A convenient starting point is the old railway station at Newent. Nearby, an embankment and abutments of a bridge mark the line, closed in 1964. The canal followed a much lower contour, actually passing beneath the road at this point. Bordered by Scots pines, the approach is typical of the Great Western Railway and leads to the station area now leased to a haulage contractor. Ahead is a sawmill once served by the railway and through trees to the right may be glimpsed remnants of Newent Ironworks, a charcoal blast-furnace in use till about 1750. The buildings have long since been converted to farming purposes.

The old line is becoming rapidly colonised by willow, hazel and ash trees as well as broom, gorse, buddleia and rosebay, and is a blaze of colour in the summer. After a few hundred yards a footpath crosses and joins the canal, now emerging from beneath the railway and bearing to the north. Near this spot it passes over the Ell Brook by a single-arched aqueduct holed in its crown to drain the water. Only a few yards away abutments of the abandoned railway bridge stand as parallel walls where it

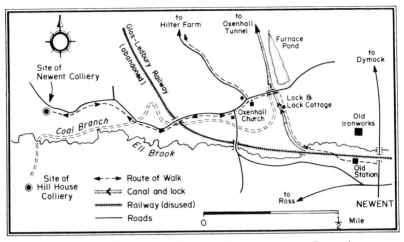

Map 4 The Hereford & Gloucester Canal: Newent to Dymock

spanned the stream. After a short distance a sudden rise in the towpath denotes a lock, although robbed of masonry for constructing the railway. In a field to the right a venerable oak was a mature tree long before the canal came, nearly two centuries ago.

A few yards further along, the next lock is typical of narrowboat practice, being only about 7ft wide. Unfortunately the ashlar masonry has fallen into very bad repair. The gates have long since gone and the chamber itself is becoming difficult to inspect due to foliage. Nevertheless, this represents the sole surviving example out of over twenty that the canal boasted, all others having succumbed to the railway or more recent developments. It is overlooked by Lock Cottage, a brick dwelling in the Palladian style built to Ballard's designs in 1838. Before then, it is doubtful whether the impoverished company had constructed a single building; a recent claim that a brick shed near Ledbury originated in the 1790s as a purpose-built barracks has not been substantiated.

On a low hill stands Oxenhall Church with its truncated spire, and a little further along the towpath a country lane crosses where once was a swing or lift bridge, of which the canal had many. The large sheet of water to the right is Furnace Pond, made in the seventeenth century for the ironworks. On the other side of the canal the sole branch left the main line,

66

curving round below the church to collieries a mile away. This was the Oxenhall Coal Branch, which lasted only a few years, its course being revealed by a steep bank and boundary fence. In the field adjoining, I discovered a fine middle stone-age axe head a year or two ago.

Further remnants of the branch can be followed by passing the church and taking a road signposted 'Gorsley'. After a minute or two a bridge over the old railway is reached, and if the parapet but serves to lean upon and ponder, it serves a useful purpose still. From this point can be seen the course of the line climbing northwards to avoid Oxenhall Tunnel, the track-bed now restored to agriculture. Bordering a wide flat area the hump of the branch where it crossed a stream distinctly appears, and a sweeping curve beyond is marked by a short hedge. On a lower horizon, vestiges of another and much earlier watercourse are also discernible in the shadows of an evening sun, excavated to feed the pond for the ironworks.

Continue along the Gorsley road for a quarter of a mile; on the left near the top of a steep descent are old shafts and a grassy dump denoting the remains of Newent Colliery which enjoyed a brief existence before succumbing in 1880. It was the last serious attempt at mining in the district. The coal branch ended near Hill House Colliery to the south, but little or nothing survives of either in this vicinity. On retracing our steps, we can either return to the main line of canal near Furnace Pond, and follow the towpath towards the tunnel, or turn left at the church to omit this section, which is rather badly overgrown. The latter course is recommended, and from the rising aspect of the road, the dome-like form of May Hill can be seen to the south. In that direction lies the ill-fated coal country that tempted the canal promoters to forsake their original course up the Leadon Valley, in favour of the crippling expense of the Oxenhall route. To the right of the road extensive orchards recently re-established are reminders of Newent's earlier fame as a cider- and perry-producing region.

Past Hilter Farmhouse a narrow sunken lane leads down to the canal. The towpath here is overgrown, but a footpath through a gate just before the bridge runs alongside the cutting, barely visible behind a screen of trees and bushes. Where this line of foliage ends is the tunnel entrance. The tunnel and many

other features are illustrated in my book *The Hereford &
Gloucester Canal.*

The footpath deviates towards a gate leading into Holder's
Lane. The barge horses went this way whilst the boatmen legged
through 2,192yd of dripping blackness, scarcely 9ft wide and
without room to pass. Not until 1849, when trade began to
improve, were regulations introduced to control passage between certain hours; how boatmen knew the time has not been
recorded; perhaps each end was permanently manned.

As you walk up the lane past Holder's Farm, banks of New
Red Sandstone confine the way, worn down by centuries of
traffic. The tunnel runs parallel, and where the road levels out a
turning to the right descends to Waterdines, a solitary house
where in the 1790s a steam pumping engine laboured nearby to
keep the tunnel excavations free of water. More than twenty
shafts were sunk along its course, none of which remains open.

Towards the end of Holder's Lane is a single-storey brick
building close to the road, which served as a blacksmith's shop
until World War I. The lane climbs steeply to the highest point
where behind a house a large grassy tip signifies the site of the
deepest shaft. Here are splendid views of the Malvern Hills, rising to over 1,400ft. Looking north and south down into the
plains below, we can appreciate the folly of this route, which
might have been avoided altogether to great advantage. Turning left at the end of the road, we proceed to just beyond two
pairs of cottages where power lines cross. Here, a field gate leads
to a footpath towards Boyce Court, its white facade a landmark
denoting the course of the canal. This was the home of John
Moggridge, Lord of the Manor of Dymock, who, with Richard
Perkins of Newent, formed a company to exploit the local coal
mines, quarries and other resources.

The path closely follows the power lines, veering to the right
at the end of the field, beyond which it passes a semi-derelict
farmstead. From the buildings two large grassy spoil mounds
some fifty yards apart can plainly be seen, evidence of the
canal's subterranean course. Close by is a strong reminder of a
more modern form of transport, the M50 motorway. In the distance a road bridge will be noticed supported by an open arch,
like a tangent upon a semi-circle—a form pleasing enough to the
eye but anathema to any self-respecting engineer.

The footpath follows alongside the motorway until reaching a concrete underpass, in form a replica of the canal tunnel and only a little narrower. The tunnel itself emerges beyond, where a stile into a wood takes us to a small brick bridge devoid of parapets across a track leading the barge horses down to the deep and mysterious cutting below. In this vicinity the path has eroded away but, from a vantage point further along the top, the tunnel portal is visible among the trees. It is now in very poor repair, and there is a blockage not very far inside.

The next quarter of a mile, where the canal winds a serpentine course through ancient woodland, is a haven for wildlife and a paradise for naturalists. It must have been more than welcome for bargemen after hours of toil working through from Oxenhall. In spring the banks are yellow with the wild daffodil so common in this region. Trees include yew, wild cherry, ash, oak, birch, sweet chestnut, hazel, may, holly and sycamore, and there is so much water in this stretch that it is hard to believe that no boat has disturbed its tranquillity for a hundred years.

Further along the top of the cutting a small stream coming in from the right has excavated a kind of canyon through marls of the Old Red Sandstone, interrupting progress and inviting a descent to the towpath. The stream was originally channelled in a leat for about fifty yards before being conducted in a cut-and-cover brick culvert down to water level. This can still be traced, and I have not encountered similar features elsewhere on this canal.

The towpath leads to a fine bridge, partly obscured by ivy, taking a carriage road to Boyce Court. It probably dates from Ballard's time when he had visions of an eventual conversion to a railway, but the insurance never paid returns. Apart from a short distance, the course beyond Boyce Court has reverted to agriculture, and it is best to follow the lane over the bridge to the Dymock road, passing the track of the railway in the process. A little to the north, the latter rejoined the canal and thereafter obscured its course more or less the whole way to Ledbury. However, just before Dymock where the road comes close to the railway embankment passing over a stream, a substantial culvert in local stone probably dates from canal days.

A further quarter of a mile brings us to the village where a modern housing development occupies the station site; from the bridge over the line the old platform is still visible below. Thus the canal walk ends as it began, with the railway, and it is interesting to note that, although a newer form of transport usurped an older, at least in this delightful backwater of Gloucestershire it did not last as long.

11 THE LEOMINSTER CANAL ·
Adrian Russell
Newnham to Southnet (5 miles)

This walk is along a fascinating stretch of abandoned canal traversing delightful Herefordshire countryside. The total distance is about five miles, although you will want to visit other parts of the canal as well, if you become as absorbed in the subject as I did. Using sheet 138 of the 1:50,000 Ordnance Survey map, you start at grid reference SO 643695 and finish at SO 673705; both these points are on a bus route along the A456.

Let us begin with a brief historical background. In his *Leominster Guide* of 1808, Jonathan Williams wrote:

> The whole line presents a romantic and picturesque appearance, sometimes gliding quietly through a level country, at other times hanging by the sides of hills, now hiding itself underground and now rolling its waters over subjected rivers; at length descending into the Severn by seventeen locks and thereby opening a communication with EVERY PART OF THE WORLD.

In fact, the canal—fully known as the Kington, Leominster & Stourport—was never completed. The intention was to link the town of Kington to the main waterway network at Stourport on the Severn, a distance of 45 miles, but only the 18 miles from Leominster to Southnet Wharf were finished. The Act for the canal was passed in 1791; the engineer was Thomas Dadford, junior, who unfortunately became overcommitted with canal undertakings at this time. The length from Southnet Wharf to Woofferton Wharf was opened in 1794 and from Woofferton to Leominster two years later, after delays in the construction of Putnal Fields Tunnel. The main cargo was coal, brought to the canal by tramroad from collieries at Pensax and Mamble.

The canal was a commercial disaster; its estimated construction costs were vastly exceeded and it never paid a single dividend. John Rennie, called in to help in emergency, criticised the design of the tunnels and aqueducts. It closed in 1858, being sold to the Shrewsbury & Hereford Railway Company for

71

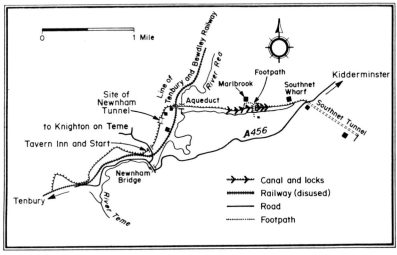

Map 5 The Leominster Canal: Newnham to Southnet

a mere £12,000, £16 for each £100 share. It was a sad ending to the optimism of the Canal Age.

The walk begins at Newnham Bridge, a small village on the A456, three miles east of Tenbury Wells. Take the Knighton-on-Teme road west of the bridge where the A456 crosses the River Rea. A short distance up the hill is The Tavern Inn; the area around the car park is the site of Newnham Wharf. West of the inn the metalled lane takes the line of the towpath; the canal is on the right, incorporated into gardens. A canalside cottage with unusual brick piers bears a datestone of 1827; of similar design to cottages on the Hereford & Gloucester Canal it is possibly by the same architect or builder. The property is identified on a copy of an old map on display at The Salway Arms at Woofferton, where it is called the Nail House. The canal runs adjacent to the back of another cottage, apparently dated 1816.

Continue over the gate and through a field and the cutting is clearly defined on your left. It opens out to form a large winding hole where the 70ft x 6ft 10in horse-drawn boats would have turned after leaving Newnham Wharf. Now the canal has been incorporated into the garden of New House and, if you cross the approach road in front of you, the canal bed can be seen 'hanging by the side of the hill' as it follows the contour around Stipers

72

Hill. Following the contours in this way reduced the number of locks needed but greatly increased the mileage. This is the furthest westward point you reach on this walk. Retrace your steps to The Tavern Inn, take refreshment if the time is right, and prepare for the main part of your excursion. Remember to keep to public footpaths; there is private property in close proximity to much of your track.

Across the Knighton-on-Teme road the canal runs parallel to the drive to Oxnalls Farm. The embankment is covered by a lush sward; the bed is often occupied by sheep, grazing innocent of the fact that boats once voyaged here. A tributary of the River Rea passes under the canal through a stone culvert. Beyond the point where the farm drive veers right and through a gate is the site of Newnham Tunnel, 94yd long, collapsed and filled in although part of the arch is believed to be intact. This tunnel was not on Dadford's original plan, where a cutting was intended. The canal course leads clearly through Tunnel Coppice and across a field to the backs of two small brick cottages, the further one of which is believed to have formed part of a small agricultural wharf. To keep to the footpath, walk behind the picturesque black-and-white cottage and through the gate alongside the wood. The canal bed comes in from the right; follow it by crossing a stile on the left and continue through the wood to the track which used to carry the Tenbury to Bewdley Railway. This is the line that goes through Newnham and keeps close to the canal, sometimes coinciding with it until it reaches the still working Shrewsbury–Hereford line at Woofferton.

Crossing the railway track, you find yourself on an obvious embankment that soon brings you to the magnificent single-arch aqueduct over the Rea. Unlike some of the other engineering features on the canal, this was a remarkably solid feat of construction, believed to have contained one million bricks made at a specially built brickworks a short distance to the south-east. In its day it was the widest single-arch aqueduct with a span of 45ft, carrying the canal 40ft above the river. Now mature trees are prising their way through the brickwork. Notice the use of solid timber to support the canal bed, and the metal star-shaped straps giving added strength. The width of the aqueduct is considerable when compared to the width of the

The aqueduct over the Rea on the Leominster Canal *(A. J. Russell)*

canal trough and much of this top area would have been filled with puddled clay to prevent leakage. To the east is a winding hole where boats unloaded coal from Mamble for the brick kilns when the aqueduct was being built, and where later they could wait for oncoming traffic to pass.

Beyond the aqueduct is a stretch of beautiful undulating countryside, small in scale and giving a feeling of complete seclusion, populated, it seems, only by birds and scampering rabbits. Below to your right is the Marl Brook, which supplied the canal with water at Southnet Wharf and is now on its way to the Rea.

As you approach a spinney, a rise in the towpath indicates the first evidence of a lock. You have been walking along the bottom level of the canal; from here it rises through seven locks, each of 6ft, to Southnet Wharf. In all, there were sixteen locks on the canal but few traces are left; the masonry has been removed over the years by local farmers. You pass the sites of two more locks and then follow a footpath past the front of Marlbrook House, an elegant equestrian centre. Along the drive are the remains of a bridge and you may discern traces of its original arch. The canal course is too overgrown to be rejoined here so it is best to return towards the house and take the track on the right which leads you to Lock House. This has been tactfully extended in recent years and retains much of its original canal character. In the cellars the lock-keeper's tools and other equipment used to be kept.

Continue past the sites of four more locks to reach the end of your walk, Southnet Wharf. The Wharf House with its bowed projections dominates the scene. The front room on the first floor was the canal company's main office and on either side of the front door were docks where boats were stored and repaired. All the older buildings here were connected with the canal. The Marl Brook feeder stream is now incorporated into the canal bed and has been landscaped into a beautiful water garden. In the basin here boats took on coal brought by tramroad from the Mamble collieries, and pieces of coal and tramroad track often turn up in the house grounds. This would have been a busy place indeed 180 years ago. A few yards more will bring you to the A456 and a bus stop close by. If you have time, however, there is more for you to see.

Southnet Tunnel, at 1,250yd the longest completed on the canal, collapsed soon after it was finished in 1795. It seems never to have been used and three workmen were killed during its construction. Thomas Jenkins was the unfortunate contractor; another of his tunnels on the Salisbury & Southampton Canal was abandoned uncompleted. The whereabouts of the west portal of the tunnel remains a mystery. Some maps show it on the Wharf House side of the main road but on the ground the far side looks more likely. Possibly the portal was destroyed during road construction. Cherry Tree Cottage by the road used to be a smithy and it is likely that this and the recently modernised cottage further up the hill were once part of the canal scene.

You may follow the line of the tunnel by veering left into Ash Coppice past the side of Cherry Tree Cottage. Mounds you see as you climb indicate spoil heaps. A large depression, partly filled with rubbish, is probably the site of a ventilation shaft. Continue through an old gate, across a pasture field and through another gate into woodland. Soon you emerge into the open near the summit of the hill; the overhead power lines are close to the line of the tunnel. Enjoy the splendid view east to the Severn where the canal was intended to lead. Carry on around the left of the next spinney and through a field; at a point about fifty yards to the right of the power lines is the east portal of the tunnel. This is a sad relic which probably never saw a single boat. The tall, narrow arch of the portal is typical of the tunnel work on this canal. Seek permission from the nearby house if you wish to examine the portal closely. The canal cut is visible for a short distance, and from then on no significant works were done. A further tunnel was planned at Pensax which, with a length of 3,850yd, would have been the longest on the canal system at that time, and a further seventeen locks were planned to descend to the Severn.

Other items of interest which may be visited on separate occasions include some lengths of canal to the west of Newnham Bridge and the only remaining overbridge, the Easton Court Bridge just north of Little Hereford. A footpath along the old railway track beside a stream about a mile east of Woofferton leads to an obvious stretch of embankment curving towards the site of the largest usable engineering work on the canal, the Teme Aqueduct. This was similar in style to the Rea Aqueduct but had three arches; it was blown up in a wartime exercise, offering much resistance. At Woofferton near The Salway Arms is a wharf and the site of six locks. On the lane to Orleton on the A49, a few yards beyond the railway bridge, is the Putnal Fields Tunnel. Both portals are accessible, on either side of the road. There is a beautiful watered stretch to the south. The Leominster Wharf House is on the A49 about one and a half miles from the town centre; this is the last significant canal feature, although some cutting was begun on the Kington–Leominster stretch. The remaining engineering works on the Leominster Canal are slowly crumbling to decay; it may not be long before they will endure only in the memories of those who have seen them.

12 THE SOUTH OXFORD CANAL ·
D. Marcus Potts
Fenny Compton to Cropredy (7½ miles)

The warm amber of Hornton Stone, the green of field and tree or the stewed tea of murky canal water—for many, the South Oxford Canal is the most picturesque of England's waterways. Admittedly there are none of the magnificent engineering masterpieces that draw thousands to the last miles of the Llangollen Canal, nor are there any of those awesome flights of locks which feature in many other canals in this up-and-down country of ours. Nevertheless, the South Oxford calls back countless visitors every year and, it is to be hoped, will continue to do so for many more to come.

But, sadly, the South Oxford Canal is almost impossible to walk! Throughout its entire length the towpath is in an atrocious condition and to find a stretch of even two or three miles passable in all weathers is very difficult. Choosing a walk of any decent length has therefore necessitated leaving the towpath occasionally, but this should not detract from the pleasure or the canal interest gained from following the South Oxford Canal between Fenny Compton and Cropredy.

The X59 Oxford–Coventry (via Banbury) bus serves both villages and stops not far from the old wharf at Fenny Compton, where ex-working narrow boats may still occasionally be seen and The George and Dragon pub backs onto the towpath. Begin by heading off westwards along the newly resurfaced towpath which serves the popular overnight moorings just here. The general conditions here are good and it is not long before the watery expanse of Fenny Compton Marina is reached. This is the home of Fenny Marine, hundreds of moored boats and over a mile of jetties. The shop stocks all the usual goods as well as an excellent *Waterways World* cruising guide to the canal.

For 600yd the towpath forms a narrow isthmus alongside the canal, crossing the inlet to the marina on a wooden footbridge, before the development of a shallow cutting signifies the approach of Fenny Compton Tunnel. That this is still called a tunnel is a piece of anachronistic nostalgia, since there has been

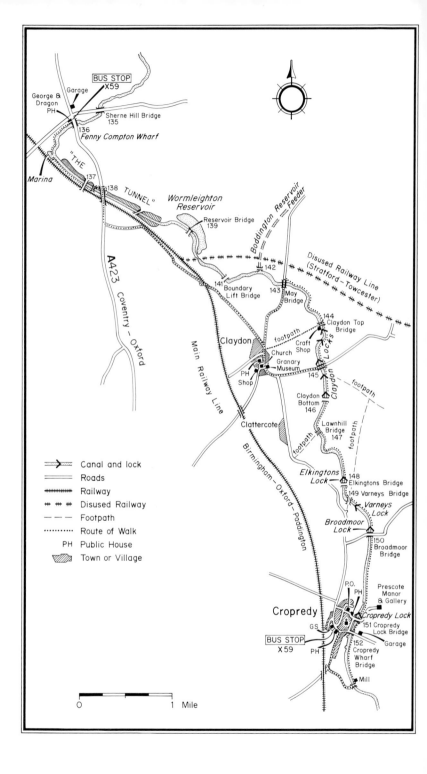

no tunnel here for over a hundred years. When the canal was first opened through to Banbury in 1778 there was indeed a tunnel which, at 1,138yd, would rank as the twelfth longest in Britain if it were still navigable today. But with construction dating from the very early days of canal engineering the tunnel had a very small bore (less than 12ft high and 9ft wide) which not only made it particularly claustrophobic but also a severe handicap to the busy traffic which soon developed on the canal. Unfortunately, the land above the tunnel had not been purchased by the canal company and it was over fifty years before the owners, Christ Church, Oxford, could be persuaded to sell up, so allowing the company to open out a central passing place in 1840. The two tunnels thus formed remained for another thirty years before further pressure from dissatisfied traders forced their complete removal in 1870, though the outline of these two isolated portions is readily discernible today.

Our walk takes us along the more northern and clearer defined of the two, past the site of a recently stabilised landslip and over the canal on perhaps the most quaint and least photographed of cast-iron turnover bridges. There are several of these on the Oxford Canal dating from the mid-nineteenth century, when a considerable modernisation programme, principally involving the northern section of the canal, bypassed 14 meandering miles by driving straight through low hills in cuttings and over shallow valleys on embankments.

Beyond the A423 road bridge the towpath disappears completely and does not return for well over a mile, by which time it is isolated and difficult to reach on foot. But just through the bridge a steepish path with earthen steps climbs up to the main road and affords an excellent view along the entire length of the tunnel.

Proceed south for 400yd and then take the minor road off to the left signposted 'Claydon'. This road, little broader than a farm track, twists and turns almost as keenly as Brindley's Oxford Canal before it arrives in Claydon a mile and a half later. You can take the first left on entering the village and return to the canal at Hay's Bridge, number 143, but Claydon is such a charming outpost of the Cotswolds that it would be a crime to

Map 6 The South Oxford Canal: Fenny Compton to Cropredy

pass it by. Centred around a quaint yellow-stoned church, whose faceless clock strikes the hours, are The Sunrising Inn and the fascinating Granary Museum. The former serves an excellent pint of Hook Norton while the latter contains an intriguing collection of artefacts and bygones from the rural life of ages past. Admission is free and both are well worth visiting. Leaving Claydon in the direction of Cropredy continue straight on at the road junction (Cropredy signposted right) and descend the slight hill, rejoining the canal at Bridge 145 overlooking Claydon Middle Lock. The route to Cropredy lies to the right, but before heading that way it is a good idea to walk briefly northwards to visit the top lock in this flight of five.

Around the lock stands the haphazard collection of old stables and maintenance buildings which for so many years evoked longing in the hearts of passing canal enthusiasts. The total absence of vehicle access or basic services, however, meant that the buildings remained untenanted and unused for almost half a century.

During that time several buildings disappeared, including the lock-keeper's cottage, which stood across the lock from the stables (the foundations can still be traced), and in more recent times vandalism began to take its toll. The blacksmith's shop survived complete with hearth and bellows well into the late seventies but was an early casualty to thoughtless destruction, though foresight saved the bellows which are now on show fully restored in the Waterways Museum at Stoke Bruerne. After countless proposals had surfaced and sank, it came as a relief when Claydon Crafts was established in 1980. They have succeeded in renovating part of the old stable block to house a shop stocking all manner of crafts, from traditional canal ware to corn dollies. The carpenters' workshops have also been restored so that the buzz of the saw and the chip of the chisel have returned once more to Claydon Top Lock. Plans may change, however, and sadly the site may again fall quiet in 1984.

Returning down the flight and passing beneath the road which led us out of Claydon takes us to the bottom of the Claydon locks and the start of the Mile Pound. To begin with the towpath is excellent and the walking good; bulrushes and reeds fringe the water's edge and the canal, at this point raised on a humble embankment, forges dead ahead for about five hundred yards. A partially silted winding hole heralds the bend into Lawnhill Bridge and what will be, during some months of the year, the site of our second departure from the towpath. Check through the bridge first because it is frequently possible to walk this next section, but if defeated by the undergrowth make your way up onto the bridge, cross the canal and follow the track back to the metalled road. Turn left and proceed for three-quarters of a mile. It is necessary to continue out of sight of Elkington's Lock and return to the canal via the bridleway that leads down to Varney's Bridge, number 149. The entrance to the path is marked by a bend in the road, an area of concrete and two tubular-steel farm gates. The bridge is easily visible from the first of these.

For those willing to risk the towpath (and I have walked it several times without mishap) there is the rest of the Mile Pound to negotiate. Having left Claydon Bottom on the straight, the canal undergoes a series of quite tight S-bends before rounding the final right-hander to line up on Elkington's Lock. The freshwater crayfish *Astacus pallipes* is common in these waters and I have frequently found their crusty remains lying starkly white in the long grass.

On the offside stands Forge Farm and the site of Clattercote Wharf. For a long time this ramshackle array of brick, stone and a splattering of mortar stood derelict, but the buildings are currently experiencing a new lease of life. Elkington's Lock continues the canal's descent to the River Cherwell and represents one of the trio of locks known as Peter's Three, after a former lock-keeper. The middle lock, Varney's, can provide an interesting insight into old farming techniques and the effect the canal must have had on the landscape. Stand high on one of the balance beams and examine the undulations of the old ridge and furrow as it ripples across the field above the lock. Then look over the towpath hedge and compare the pattern on that side. The two line up, which explains the need for an accommodation bridge above the lock.

At Broadmoor Lock, the last of these three and once the location for Peter's lock-cottage, are the remains of a wharf and, reputedly, some lime kilns. Below the lock the idyllic positioning of Fisherman's Cottage blends with the sight of Cropredy Church on the approaching skyline. This stretch is indeed very popular with fishermen and, having witnessed the capture of some carp of over 20lb, I can fully appreciate why.

The narrows of a long-removed lift bridge mark your arrival in the village, and the line of moored boats confirms Cropredy's status as one of the best known and most popular of canalside villages. Visible through the trees to the east is Prescote Manor. From Cropredy Lock walk up onto the canal bridge and along Red Lion Street to the elbow in the road, where a small cast-iron gate leads into the churchyard. The Red Lion itself was made famous by L.T.C. Rolt and E. Temple Thurston in their books *Narrow Boat* and *The Flower of Gloster*.

The grand scale of the church bears witness to Cropredy's former importance, while within are some interesting relics from the village's turbulent past. On 29 June 1644 one of the least known but none the less important Civil War battles was fought around Cropredy's bridge over the River Cherwell. Despite vastly inferior numbers, the Royalists won a considerable victory. They captured the parliamentarian artillery and scattered the troops, leaving a sheepish General Waller to explain his loss to Cromwell. In spite of the victory it is debatable whether the Royalists gained any advantage since, some would say, it was as a direct result of this disaster that Cromwell chose to found the New Model Army that eventually defeated King Charles. Some pieces of armour are displayed in the church and the brass lectern has one bronze foot—ask a local why!

Leaving the churchyard by the west gate, make for the High Street and turn left by the telephone kiosk. Follow the road round to the left, through the square and to The Brasenose Inn. The bus stops over the road from the pub, but if you have time to spare do follow the road down to the left and return to the canal at Bridge 153. From the bridge it is possible to look back to Cropredy Lock, with the old coal wharf on the left (though no longer recognisable as such) and the toll-house narrows where working boats were gauged in the foreground. Overlooking the canal 200yd south is the original Manor House. This largely sixteenth-century stone building still boasts the moat which once connected with the River Cherwell via a short arm. The canal severed this link but the channel formed by the newer union offers useful private moorings today. A short walk beyond stands the scarred shell of Cropredy Mill, victim of a disastrous fire in 1892 and, more recently, considerable attention from local vandals. From the bridge which stands beside it a combination of farm track and road leads back to the village via Bourton House, the village school and Station Road, so ending a walk of about seven and a half miles.

13 THE PEAK FOREST CANAL ·
Michael Miller
Whaley Bridge to Marple (7 miles)

This walk takes you along a rural, but not remote, canal. It perches on the hillside above the Goyt valley, offering some good open views. At the Whaley Bridge end it is closely and noisily accompanied by the A6, but the road soon moves a tolerable distance away. The canal runs in a broadly south-east to north-west direction, a factor to be taken into consideration with the weather forecast. I made the mistake of walking into a strong northwesterly wind on a day interspersed with hail showers and now have a fair idea how it feels to be shot blasted! You can travel from one end to the other by rail. The stations at Marple and Whaley Bridge are each within a few hundred yards of the canal but are on different lines, the connection being made by an easy fifteen minute walk from New Mills Central (from Marple) to New Mills Newtown (for Whaley Bridge). Emerging from Whaley Bridge station, cross the main road and turn left down a lane parallel to the A6. In a few yards you reach the terminal basin. A brief exploration of this is recommended before commencing your walk. Note the warehouse at the end. Presently occupied by Coles Morton Marine, it was originally built in 1832 by the Cromford and High Peak Railway to act as a transhipment dock from boat to wagon.

The railway was built as a cheaper alternative to a canal rising to a 1,200ft summit level to make a link between the Peak Forest Canal and the Cromford Canal 33 miles to the south-east. This opened a through route between Manchester and Nottingham rather shorter and quicker than via the heavily congested Trent & Mersey Canal through the Potteries. The railway was originally worked by horse-drawn wagons on level sections interspersed with inclined planes up which the wagons were hauled by stationary steam-engines. Latterly operated with locomotives, the railway closed in 1967. South of Buxton the High Peak Trail is now a public walkway worth exploring in its own right. The old steam-engine at Middleton, now demonstrated worked by compressed air, is notable as is Sheep Pasture incline

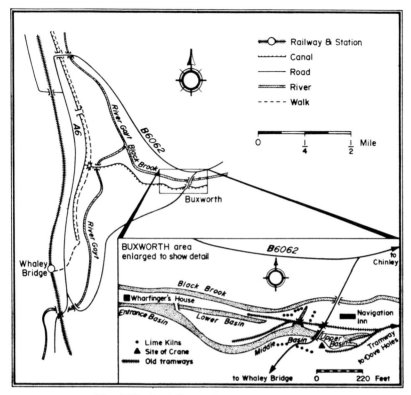

Map 7 The Peak Forest Canal near Whaley Bridge

leading down to the transhipment wharf at High Peak Junction south of Cromford.

Begin the walk by turning right, keeping the basin on your left. A wooden walkway carries you above an overflow weir at the far end of the basin so taking you on to the canal proper. Here the towpath is somewhat uneven but for the rest of the way it is smooth going. Soon views open up to the right over the Goyt Valley, and the embankment carrying the Buxworth arm over the river is visible ahead. Buxworth was once Bugsworth but a local vicar who disliked the name had it changed in 1930.

Half a mile from the terminus the junction with the arm is reached, and here you have a choice of crossing on the modern high level footbridge or descending the fine cobbled ramp to the right to go under the arm through a splendid masonry mini-aqueduct and up the corresponding ramp to the left. The tow-path continues ahead but you may wish, if time permits, to turn right and explore the half-mile arm leading to the disused Buxworth Basin. In doing so you will be walking what was originally the main line and discovering the reason for building a canal that seems to have no particular purpose in going where it does.

The Peak Forest Canal was built as an extension to the Ashton Canal in order to tap the limestone quarries at Doveholes. Authorised in 1794, the canal was open throughout by 1804. It terminated in a complex of wharves and basins at Bugsworth, the connection with the quarries being made by a 5½ mile tramway which climbed almost 600ft, 209ft of this being accomplished by an inclined plane near Chapel-en-le-Frith. Wagons brought limestone down to the basin where it was loaded into boats, much of it after being crushed or burnt in lime kilns. At one time, in the 1880s, over 600 tons a day were shipped out, coal for the kilns providing a back load for the flotilla of narrow boats.

Railway competition had already affected the canal revenues. In 1846 the navigation was permanently leased to the Sheffield,

A woodland scene on the Peak Forest Canal *(M. G. Miller)*

Ashton-under-Lyne and Manchester Railway, the forerunner of the Great Central. Its Victorian heyday over, the canal went into decline as did the tramway. The kilns went out of use in 1915 and the tramway ceased operation in 1926; the basins fell into disuse and the arm was eventually closed off.

Far from being the end of the story, the basin's closure has offered a new beginning. In 1967 the Inland Waterways Protection Society came into being with the purpose of restoring the basin. Slowly this aim is being achieved. It was consequently very pleasing the day I walked the canal to find the stop planks removed, the first basin full of water and forty-four boats moored there and along the arm. I was told that ninety boats were expected for the weekend rally. Even on 'waterless' weekends the derelict basins are fascinating to explore from the wharfinger's house by the gauging lock to the remains of the crane and covered dock at the far end. Despite the inappropriateness of its sign showing a ship in full sail, The Navigation pub is worth a visit, not only for refreshment but also to study the old photographs of the basin in use. Copies of Brian Lamb's booklet *The Peak Forest Canal and Tramway* can also be bought there.

Returning to the walk, just beyond the junction you will find a stone milepost by the towpath marking 14 miles from the junction with the Ashton Canal at Dukinfield. Full miles are denoted by thick stones (ie about 8in) with thin ones for half-miles. Very shortly a modern steel lift bridge and accompanying high level footbridge are reached. Inspection of the masonry of the bridge narrows shows the original crossing to have been by a swing bridge.

The civil engineering involved in constructing the canal on an artificial ledge cut into the hillside, especially where this is steep, is most impressive, particularly when it is remembered that knowledge of soil science was rudimentary and there were no mechanical aids; all the earth-moving was done by the labour of the 'navigators' using pick and shovel. A hillside location meant that a breach was a constant possibility. Note the precautions: the grooves for stop planks to be inserted to form a temporary dam so that the section of canal could be drained for repair or maintenance by opening a valve. Along this section, before the hump-backed Bridge 33, a small iron roller is set at the edge of the channel. Holes in each end allowed bars to be inserted to turn it. A chain (now missing) would thereby have been wound onto the roller. The other end of the chain would have been attached to a wooden trap-door in the bed of the canal, leading to a culvert. Examine the embankment below the roller and you will find the outlet. From time to time you will also cross overflow weirs designed to carry off floodwater.

After another lift bridge and a sewage works, an ugly concrete bridge marks Furness Vale. The railway has accompanied the canal closely from Whaley Bridge; trains stop at Furness Vale and there is a pub here. You cross a small aqueduct and pass an old wharf before finding another milepost near a marina. The hillside opens out on the left and there is a fine view to the right of the railway viaduct crossing the Goyt before New Mills. Beyond Bridge 29 the Ladyline boatyard on the offside has an old crane on its wharf. The name New Mills is now seen to be appropriate, the canal being lined with old factory buildings. The next bridge, with a stone milepost by it, is built on the skew. On early canals crossings were invariably at right angles, but as the engineers' skill developed so they were able to construct bridges crossing at an angle. Note how the courses of masonry are set at an angle to produce the appropriate line.

Beyond the town is an attractive wooded section. The next bridge, Green's Hall Bridge, is also very pleasing, but after Bridge 26 there are houses with untidy gardens coming down to the canal. These do not extend far, however; a short but high embankment carries the canal over a stream, an original swing bridge is passed, the hillside becomes very steep as the river and canal swing near each other and there are good views over the valley. Meanwhile the railway has at last set off on an independent course helping to make this a most attractive section. Beyond a swing bridge and one of arched masonry, the towpath narrows to single file. You should pause at Strines Aqueduct to admire its construction. Its outer sides are curved in plan to resist the pressure of the water in the trough. Adjacent to it an old wharf still carries the wooden post on which a crane was mounted, whilst the lane under the aqueduct is cobbled, the whole overhung by trees—a delightful spot! If need be, note that the lane leads down to Strines station about a mile away.

Bridge 22, Turflea Swing Bridge, belies its name having been converted into a steel lift bridge. From here to Marple the hill-side has occasional gorsy sections giving it a wilder aspect. Beyond the high footbridge, number 20, a half-mile stone can be found. Further on the hillside to the left has parallel ridge and furrow, the traces of medieval strip farming. The main road into Marple has now sidled up to the canal and is keeping it close company on the right even if at a lower level. The aptly named Brick Bridge has recently been rebuilt with obvious care. It is also a turnover bridge where the towpath changes sides. You are now on the outskirts of Marple and very shortly reach the junction with the Macclesfield Canal and the head of the flight of locks.

There is much to see here. Apart from the numerous moored boats, the junction bridge is a joy to behold. Designed by Telford and completed in 1831, it is almost all curves. A cobbled ramp led boathorses on to the bridge whilst a curved ramp leads down and under on the other side, the object being to enable the horse to change sides without entangling the tow-rope; note how the balustrade is carried down to ground level. From the bridge, view the repair workshop with its enclosed dock, outside staircase and covered unloading bay, before noting the commemorative plaque just beyond the bridge. This celebrates the 1974 reopening of the locks as a result of co-operative effort between the British Waterways Board and volunteer weekend 'navvies' funded by a consortium of local authorities. For over ten years the derelict locks had broken the Cheshire Ring, a hundred-mile waterway circuit. One must salute the determination and persistence of the Peak Forest Canal Society and the Inland Waterways Association who eventually won officialdom over to the idea of restoration.

The locks are magnificent. More than averagely deep, the six-teen locks drop the canal 210ft from its 506ft summit level within a mile. The top half of the flight wriggles down through the town whilst the bottom half is overhung with trees. Note the splendid stone tail bridges, and at the first road crossing use the delightful horse tunnel to cross under the road, safe from traffic. Further down, Samuel Oldknow's old cotton warehouse with its covered unloading bay (now sensitively converted into architects' offices) is notable. At the road bridge just beyond the warehouse leave the canal and turn right for Marple Station,

Entering the horse tunnel at Marple Locks, Peak Forest Canal *(M. G. Miller)*

but, if time permits, walk to the bottom of the locks to see Marple Aqueduct. Designed by Benjamin Outram, this is one of the finest masonry aqueducts in the country. It enables boats to cross the River Goyt 100ft below. Viewing it makes an impressive end to the walk and further increases your respect for the skill and boldness of those who built our canal system, creating works that were incidentally aesthetic in fulfilling their commercial function.

14 A POTTERIES WALK: CALDON, TRENT & MERSEY AND MACCLESFIELD CANALS · Neil Coates

(11 miles)

Few areas of Britain have been more intensively developed than the Potteries. Over two centuries, industrial activity has ravaged the ground, as man has delved for coal and iron and scoured immense clay pits. Manufacturing industries have polluted the air and the rivers and covered the Trent-side pastures with industrial and residential sprawl. Now many of these industries are redundant and a feeling of industrial dereliction pervades the area; until recently, the Potteries could boast the greatest concentration of derelict land in Britain. However, in the past few decades restructured old and dynamic new undertakings have been developed, together with a growing concern for the environment. This walk presents a combination of industrial history and environmental improvement for which the Potteries have become widely known. It begins at the point where the Bucknall Road crosses the Caldon Canal, some half-mile east of Hanley centre. There are frequent bus services from Hanley Bus Station. Access to the towpath is through a gap in the fencing just east of the bridge.

Start with the canal on your right, reed-fringed and peaceful. Within two hundred yards you pass by a wooden lift bridge—unusual in this area—and at once you are in the industrial Potteries. On the right is a half-demolished works; on the far side of the next bridge the canal winds through the complex of pottery factories belonging to H. and R. Johnson. On your left, the first two of a number of bottle kilns (so-called because of their shape) that you will see peer out over the top of a large corrugated steel kaolin storehouse (kaolin is China clay, used throughout the pottery industry but especially in the manufacture of porcelain). Bottle kilns, or ovens, are a survival from the heyday of the industry when over two thousand of them dominated this landscape. Now there are only perhaps fifty left, each a museum piece as stringent air quality controls make their use impossible. They were the furnaces in which the pots were fired, now replaced by huge electric ovens. Boats are still used

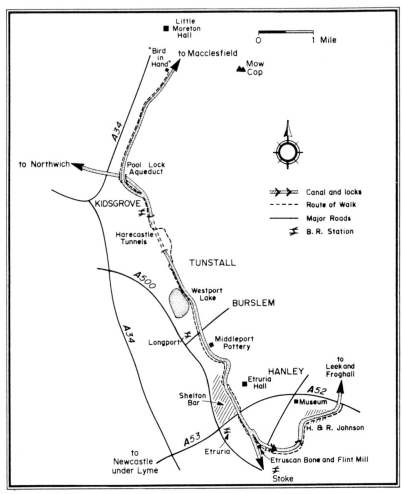

Map 8 Sections of the Caldon, Trent & Mersey and Macclesfield Canals: Hanley to Little Moreton Hall

by Johnsons to convey pots from one process to the next in their factories on either side of the canal.

The canal swings left, with the Hanley Borough Electricity Works (1894), the first in the Potteries, standing forlorn on the opposite bank. Soon reeds appear again in abundance as the canal bends right into Hanley Park. To your left is the Vale of Trent, with an industrial estate in the mid-distance, a green belt

92

reclaimed from pit spoil and marl holes and an urban–rural fringe on the horizon. Hanley Park was established in the 1890s and is a typical urban recreation area. There is no direct access from the towpath, the canal striking through the wooded greenery beneath ornate iron bridges. To visit the park, leave the towpath at the modern concrete girder bridge at the beginning of this stretch and use the entrance gates at the roadside. Refreshments and public conveniences are available. From the towpath you should see a wide variety of wildlife on the water and in the trees.

As you leave the park the surroundings abruptly change. Terraces of houses march down to the canalside, the end-terraces almost hanging over the water, reminding you of the close links between the canal and the original terrace-dwellers' livelihood. On the left is Cauldon College. Now comes the first lock on the walk, with the lock-keeper's cottage boarded up, its future uncertain. The canal horizon is dominated by a huge gas tank at Etruria gas works. You can catch a bus into Hanley by crossing the lock-gates to a stop opposite the cottage; it is a three-quarter mile ride to the splendid new museum famous for its superb collection of pottery and porcelain, and open every day except Sundays.

From the towpath, note a small warehouse with bricked up windows and doorways and the remains of a hoist. There are many of these on this walk, originally dependent on the canal for transport but later opening windows and doorways to the road and shutting off those to the canal. Soon you pass the modern Podmores Pottery Works on the right, while on the left are old terrace houses. Many of these terraces were built by pottery owners for their labourers and sited close to the works, within sound of the pottery's bell summoning them to work and within sight of the pottery clock.

Ahead are the twin pithead towers of Wolstanton Colliery, while on the canal is a two-lock staircase. To the left is a small park created on the site of a gas works which itself replaced the first North Staffordshire Infirmary. Beyond lies Etruria gas works, opened by Stanley Baldwin in 1929, and Twyfords, makers of porcelain products. To the east is Hanley, the shopping and entertainment centre of the Potteries, with the tall, dark tower of Unity House providing a focus of attention.

Now you are approaching the junction of the Caldon Canal and the Trent & Mersey. Just before you reach it, look out for a group of buildings below canal level which comprise the Etruscan Flint and Bone Mill, built in 1857 by Jesse Shirley for the roasting and crushing of flint and bone, both important in the ceramic industry for whiteners and strengthening agents. The mill is served by a short arm from the Trent & Mersey.

By the junction, cross the Trent & Mersey just above Summit Lock to join the towpath walk on the left bank. This major canal, engineered by James Brindley, was chiefly promoted by Josiah Wedgwood, whose interest was to bring quantities of kaolin from docks on the Mersey to his new works at Etruria and to provide an outlet for his wares. Following the long straight takes you beneath a new road bridge to the site of Wedgwood's first factory, opened in 1769 and closed in 1950. Only two of the original buildings remain. On the left is a building with a domed roof, now a preserved monument, but no records exist of its original function. It was built on the same level as the canal but, owing to mining subsidence, has sunk to its present level, a fate escaped by the canal through the skill of its engineers and the quality of its maintenance. For the other survivor, cross the bridge and look into the middle distance for Etruria Hall, built for Wedgwood within sight of his works. Today, much altered, it serves as offices of the British Steel Corporation.

Until the middle of the nineteenth century, landscaped gardens swept down to the Fowlea Brook and the Vale of Etruria; these were buried beneath the vast Shelton Iron and Steel Works, known as Shelton Bar, developed in the 1840s by Lord Granville. This complex has itself succumbed to the march of time; it was declared superfluous in the early 1970s and, despite vigorous protests, its production facilities were withdrawn a few years later. It is an eerie landscape through which the canal now meanders. For the next mile, the contorted remains of the giant steelworks dominate the view. Rolling mill facilities are still housed in the enormous buildings from which emanate diabolic screeches as steel is rolled, cut and shaped. Overlooking the rolling mills are the pitheads of Wolstanton Colliery, at 1,138yd the deepest in Britain. In the midst of this dereliction, pollution and industrial chaos, however, nature has retained, or perhaps regained, a foothold. Campion, wild parsley and dog daisies brighten the canal banks, there are coots, swans and gulls on the water and, along the towpath, the painted numbers are fishing peg numbers, evidence of a large fish population, mainly roach and gudgeon.

Gaunt and rusting remains of blast furnaces stand guard over rows of castings; ahead it is not a miniature nuclear power reactor that you see but the bulbous shape of a Calor gas tank. To the right of the tank the dull, sparsely vegetated spoil heaps contrast sharply with the area to the left where similar tips have been landscaped and grassed; the trees are decorative and help to consolidate the soil. Gradually the steelworks is left behind. Ahead, the settlement on the hillside is Burslem, mother town of the Potteries. You can see the floodlights of Port Vale FC, and in the foreground a marshy area is all that remains of a branch canal that once served Burslem.

As you leave the steelworks, notice the bottle oven on the right. Round a bend is the old bricked-up warehouse of the Royal Staffordshire Pottery, its narrow wharf long abandoned. Further on is another area that has recently been landscaped. Once this was a community of back-to-back houses for pottery workers; now picnic tables stand on slopes of grass and trees. The vast derelict area on the left is a site of old potteries and marl holes, whence clay was once dug, now used as a tipping ground for pottery waste, shraff, by Wedgwoods.

Nameless and gloomy buildings line the canal until you reach Middleport Pottery, a perfect working example of the many small potteries of the late eighteenth and nineteenth centuries. This is a historical monument, with its bottle oven and cobbled yard leading down to the wharves with their small cranes. Machinery is still powered by a steam-engine. Wind-blown kaolin picks out brickwork and cobbles, and old barrels packed with straw await freshly made pots.

Continue to a boatyard which occupies the site of another old pottery. A bridge built in 1856 carries the road from Longport to Burslem and Tunstall. You can refresh yourself at The Duke of Bridgwater, The Pack Horse or The Railway. Beyond the bridge, a bottle oven on the right bank faces several old buildings including a brewhouse and a pottery. A few hundred yards further on the canal forms the eastern boundary of Westport Nature Park, where a substantial lake has been created from

boggy wasteland and derelict tipping sites. In all, over a
hundred acres of parkland have been established. Wildfowl pro-
liferate here and you may see a heron or kingfisher. The lake has
been stocked with fish and is also used for a variety of
watersports. This scheme has won major European awards for
land reclamation; it was once Port Vale's football ground until
subsidence made it unplayable. On the right the terraces of
Burslem and Tunstall stride down the hill, while the hill in the
middle distance is Harecastle.

After Westport Park you enter a region of industrial desola-
tion with several overgrown canal arms leading nowhere and the
occasional derelict wharf reminding you of the once busy past.
After Bridge 129 a view opens along the straight to the south
portal of Harecastle Tunnel. To the left is the gaunt pithead
building of Chatterley mine, its arched ecclesiastical windows
expressing Victorian confidence.

Now the towpath becomes overgrown. Pass beneath the railway bridge and cross the canal at Bridge 130. From here you can
see the portals of both Harecastle tunnels. On the left is
Brindley's original bore of 1777, in length 2,880yd, and on the
right Telford's 1827 tunnel, some yards longer. Until 1918 both
tunnels were used, northbound traffic through Telford's and
southbound through Brindley's. In that year, however, subsidence caused Brindley's tunnel to be closed; the effect of subsidence on Telford's can be seen by looking at the gauge in the
tunnel entrance.

Follow the path leading up from Bridge 130 to the right of the
tunnels. The moon-like landscape that unfolds on the right is all
that remains of Goldendale Ironworks. Now you are on the
route taken by the horses while the boats were legged through
below. Your path joins Chatterley Road, which shortly turns
sharp left. Ignore this and continue into Hollywall Lane. Turn
almost immediately left and take the unnamed road up past a
small terrace of cottages. This winds its way to the top of the hill
where you can look back over the Vale of Etruria, named by
Wedgwood after the ancient Etruscan ware he admired. Your
path traverses a permanent gypsy camp, small red-brick
bungalows contrasting with chrome-bright caravans, then
becomes a pitted track to the summit by a farmyard where a
right turn takes you to Boathorse Road. Through a gap in the

hedge on the left note a memorial, reduced in height by lightning, built on Alsagers Bank to commemorate a mining disaster. Ahead you may see the flat Cheshire Plain and to the right Mow Cop dominates the skyline.

To the left as you carry on a small drift mine taps the outlying measures of the coalfield and you pass a terrace of houses roughly contemporary with the canal, and The Rifleman pub. You descend down a wooded valley, cross a main road and carry straight on along the walled and tree-lined path to emerge above the northern portal of Brindley's tunnel and the towpath on its left. Soon the canal's orange-coloured water tinted with oxide is beside you as it emerges from Telford's portal. Kidsgrove Station Bridge crosses the canal askew, its cast-iron girders lined with brick.

Suddenly the junction with the Macclesfield Canal is upon you. The Trent & Mersey continues into the Cheshire Plain and the Macclesfield leaves beneath a Trent & Mersey towpath bridge. Depending on the time, either cross this bridge and join the Macclesfield towpath, or continue past the junction to The Blue Bell or The Tavern, which both serve food. The Macclesfield, a much later canal than the Trent & Mersey, opened in 1836, winds through Pipers Boatyard and crosses the Trent & Mersey via Pool Lock Aqueduct. An optical illusion suggests it has been flowing uphill; a few hundred yards back it was on the same level as the Trent & Mersey but now it is 20ft above. Do not, however, forget the locks which have brought the Trent & Mersey down to the Cheshire Plain.

Over the aqueduct you are in Cheshire. A straight section takes you over the A50, whereupon the urban tangle is left behind and rural tranquillity unfolds. The water is comparatively clean and nothing like the colour of the Trent & Mersey, a clear indication of the effect of industry. The towpath takes you through shady cuttings; trees and sky are reflected in the water, kestrels hover above and foxes and hedgehogs may be seen.

From Bridge 94 you can reach the A34 with a large thatched pub, The Bleeding Wolf, a hundred yards to the right. Back on the towpath, note the long approach to the Macclesfield's first lock with a rise of only a few inches, a good indication of the tolerances to which the canals were constructed. By its side is a good lock-keeper's cottage.

As you approach some cottages on the left, note a sluice gate to control water level and lift your eyes to enjoy the clear view of Mow Cop, with its folly in the shape of a ruined castle. On this rugged buttress in 1807 a group of Wesleyans, dismayed at the way their church was developing, first met openly and gave rise to Primitive Methodism.

Now the walk is nearly over and the canal blends naturally into the landscape. Cows wade in the shallows opposite the towpath among reeds shaded by alder and willow, and moorhen forage in the waterside vegetation more like a village pond than an industrial canal. Compare this to the route through Shelton Bar, only five miles but seemingly a whole world away.

The end of the walk is The Bird in Hand, a small pub but in many ways a fascinating survival. It stands by the towpath next to a swing bridge. Go into the back room with its fireplace, dartboard and plain formica-topped tables and wait for your pint to be brought up in a large jug from the cellar. No music or machines disturb the conversation and there is no more suitable place to think over what you have seen on your walk.

However, if you are still energetic you can walk from here a further 1½ steep miles to the top of Mow Cop where views stretch to the Peak District, North Wales, Shropshire or to the great dish of Jodrell Bank telescope and to Manchester and the Lancashire moorlands—eight counties on a clear day. Or Little Moreton Hall, a splendid moated black-and-white Tudor mansion, is only a mile away along the A34. You can catch a bus back to Hanley close to The Bird in Hand or catch a train at Kidsgrove station to Stoke-on-Trent.

15 THE RUFFORD CANAL · Albert Cliffe
Burscough to Rufford (4½ miles)

The walk begins at Burscough where the A59 crosses the Leeds & Liverpool Canal, opposite The Admiral Lord Nelson pub. This used to be called The Packet House, after the Wigan packet which, according to the Liverpool Directory of 1790, sailed six days a week between Liverpool and Wigan. The packet called at Burscough, a well-known canal village from whose wharves goods were widely distributed. Formby Hall collected its coal from Burscough. Large manure heaps lined the canalside; horse manure was brought from Liverpool to be used on the Lancashire flatlands for the vegetables carried to Liverpool by boat. Today the British Waterways Board has a wharf, mooring site and services here.

Note the paving stones under the bridge and walk along the towpath past buildings until you reach white railings. Look for a boundary stone behind them. Continue to Junction Bridge, dating from 1816, where the Rufford Canal joins the Leeds & Liverpool. Here you can see a dry dock, old bargees' cottages, Latham Top and Latham Bottom locks and The Ship Inn, an old canal pub once known as The Blood Tub, where the local pigs were brought to be slaughtered. Soon you come to Runnel Brow Bridge and lock, pleasantly sited with recently planted trees and convenient seats; the lock and wooden overbridges are painted black and white. You may not see many boats, except in summer, but there are plenty of wild flowers to be found.

After a later railway bridge, number 2A, you reach Moss Lock, once known as Tommy Lowe's. Although the land appears flat, the canal is actually descending to the estuary of the Ribble. Away to the right are Parbold and Harrock hills, only 300 and 500ft high but looking much higher. Look for comfrey by the towpath, probably used by the boatmen in poultices for sprains. Black-headed gulls, Canada geese, shelduck and peewits are also often to be seen. German's Lock follows quickly and a bridge; the date on the keystone looks like 1829.

New lock-gates were installed in 1974 at Chicken Lock, number 6; note how the bollards have been worn by towropes.

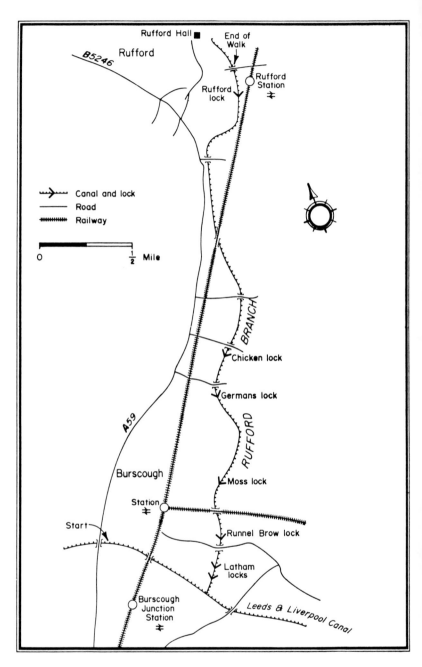

Map 9 The Rufford Canal: Burscough to Rufford

Recent sheet steel interlock piling defends the canal banks here; one mile of bank required 5,280 piles at a cost of £3 each when they were installed, although they cost much more today. Between the next bridge, Prescott Bridge, and the railway is a milestone that used to read 'Junction with Leeds & Liverpool Canal 2 miles. Tarleton 5 miles'.

The next length is tree-lined on the right and there is a fine variety of vegetation, with red campion, yellow iris, bracken and bulrushes, yellow vetch, fungi and the shells of freshwater snails. Sometimes you will see partridges scuttling into the undergrowth. The swing bridge used to be called Marsh Moss but is now Marsh Meadow, indicating a change in the character of the land. The canal bends right and the spire of Rufford Church comes into view.

Rufford Lock has new gates and stop planks with another milestone in the hedge. Then comes the rebuilt Chapel Bridge with its blue painted railings. Here you leave the canal; but if you have time it is worth walking along Diamond Jubilee Lane to Rufford Church. Seek out the sundial on the south side. Its base is an ancient cross and you might try to decipher the date. The pillar on the base was once part of the font, dating at least from 1736. There is an old gravestone by the west door and the church contains a Flaxman sculpture, an alabaster tombstone dated 1458 and other fascinating features. Rufford Old Hall, built by Thomas Hesketh (1491–1523) and now owned by the National Trust, is nearby. From Rufford there are buses every hour back to Burscough, three miles away along the main road.

16 THE SHEFFIELD & SOUTH YORKSHIRE NAVIGATION ·

Michael Miller *Rotherham to Sheffield (6 miles)*

Those who imagine all canals are remote, rural and idyllic will be in for a surprise if they walk this stretch. Reflecting the forces which brought it into being—manufacturers' demands for cheap transport—this walk traverses a largely industrial landscape. At first it keeps its distance, but as the Sheffield terminus is neared the walls of factories and steelworks close in, confining the canal to a brick-lined corridor. Despite this, or perhaps because of it, the walker has a sense of remoteness as the towpath carries him through the city along a transport route now spurned by the industry it was built to serve. Disused for commercial purposes since 1970, it is used occasionally by intrepid pleasure boaters but has a neglected, run-down feeling. However, there is much to interest the walker.

Although now all part of the Sheffield & South Yorkshire Navigation, the walk covers two sections built almost a century apart. The first was a product of the age of river improvement. After several years' struggle to defeat the opposition of landowners, the Company of Cutlers gained a Parliamentary Act in 1726 enabling them to make the River Don navigable from Doncaster to Tinsley. By 1740 boats could get up to Rotherham, and to Tinsley eleven years later, but goods to and from Sheffield still had to go overland. Eighteenth-century industrialisation and town growth led the Cutlers' Company to commission a survey in 1792 for an extension of the waterway into Sheffield, but opposition delayed successful presentation of the Bill until 1815. Four years later the four mile long canal, with twelve locks overcoming a height difference of 70ft, was opened.

Sheffield was relatively late to gain access to water transport but early to get the benefits of a railway. In 1838 trains were running between Sheffield and Rotherham. Waterway receipts fell in the face of this competition and in 1850 the canal was taken over by the South Yorkshire Railway and River Don Company which later became part of the Manchester, Sheffield

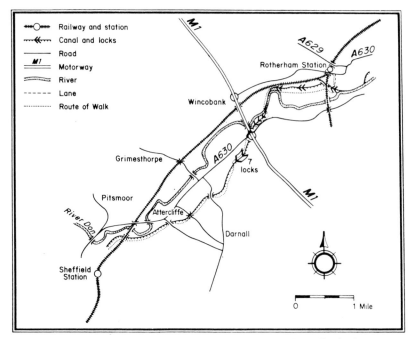

Map 10 The Sheffield & South Yorkshire Navigation: Rotherham to Sheffield

and Lincolnshire Railway. In 1894 the newly set up Sheffield & South Yorkshire Navigation bought the waterway but control was retained by the railway company which prevented improvements from being made. Nationalised in 1948, the waterway is now under the jurisdiction of the British Waterways Board and has recently been enlarged and modernised. This £16m scheme enables 700-ton barges to come up to Rotherham. However, the section covered by the walk has been left unchanged, quietly slumbering within its status as a 'remainder waterway'.

The railway may have caused problems for the waterway but it serves the walker well. Rotherham station is a convenient starting place. Turn right and follow Masbro Street as it bends to the left. Cross the main road and turn left. In a very short distance, just past The Windmill pub, turn right into a narrow lane beside Rotherham United Football Club ground. Keep straight on as the lane turns into what looks an unpromising muddy footpath passing The Slag Reduction Company and a scrap-buyer's yard.

Suddenly the scene changes. In front is a bridge crossing the tail of Ickles Lock. By the lock is a well-kept house with neat lawns; the lock too is sprucely painted, the scene marred only by a wrecked car at the water's edge. Downstream, to the left, the River Don joins the navigation but the lock marks the tail end of an artificial cut bypassing the river. Crossing the bridge and turning right you find yourself on a wide grassy towpath. To the left, cranes with huge electromagnets move scrap metal but somehow the towpath has a sense of remoteness from it all. Despite some miscellaneous plastic flotsam, the waterway is in good condition. Pussy willow grows by the path and moorhens paddle amongst the reeds.

The next lock, Holmes Lock, is deep. It has a rise of 9ft and is often full to overflowing, creating a waterfall at its lower gates. Cross the bridge at its tail and rejoin the towpath. Once past the works on the right, civilisation recedes and in the relative silence birdsong is clear.

Soon after passing the cut-off abutments of a demolished railway bridge, you see a small water channel to the right of the towpath. This is Holmes Goit which once fed the water-wheels of Walkers at Holmes Works, Masborough. The Goit parallels the canal, turning the towpath into a causeway. Gardens come down to the Goit; in one an unfinished boat hull is propped up, whilst horses graze in an adjoining field. Approaching the next lock, depending on wind direction, you may become aware that a sewage works is not far away, an occupational hazard to those who walk river valleys near towns.

By contrast with the previous one, Jordans Lock is shallow, the rise being less than 2ft. It marks the end of the artificial cut, a huge horseshoe weir leading down to the river. It also marks the end of Holmes Goit, and to follow the towpath you will need to cross the 10-in wide metal sluice gate to the right, at the head of the leat. To the right a wooded hillside rises steeply, whilst ahead are distant views of Tinsley Viaduct and beyond of Wincobank, a hill surmounted by a prehistoric earthwork. Curving sharply left past the unprotected weir, the river takes the walker under a railway bridge and past sewage works to left and right.

The scene is now more industrial with views of steelworks to the left and a power station to the right near the viaduct. By the river are several cast-iron bollards, a reminder of its commercial past. Bridges carrying pipes and cables are followed by a new railway bridge near a signal box labelled 'Tinsley East Jc'. Shortly the river swings off to the right, the towpath crossing it on a long concrete footbridge taking you to the bottom lock of the Tinsley flight.

This is a pleasant spot, fairly enclosed, well kept and with a bench to sit on. Cross the swing bridge at the head of the lock. The next lock is not far above it; although the sound of traffic on the M1 is apparent, the canal shows how attractive an urban waterway can be. The channel is in good condition, the towpath is gravelled, rubbish is minimal, surrounding slopes are grassed and benches provided. At the next lock there is street access and the towpath crosses to the right-hand side via a bridge at its tail. Below to the right is the river, soon to be finally lost to sight; note the overflow weir crossed by the towpath.

The two-tier Tinsley Viaduct carrying the M1 and the A630 now looms overhead. Beyond it Hadfield's steelworks are to the right, together with the cooling towers of the power station. Further on are more steelworks from both private and public sector, Edgar Allen and BSC. The road bridge below the next lock gives access to Sheffield Road and to The Plumpers pub together with an adjoining café.

The intervening pound before the next lock is rather longer, and as you walk it you may be puzzled by a low length of brick wall capped with stone on the offside. If you study it, you will see it is actually one side of a lock chamber. It marks the site of a lock removed when a new railway bridge was built in 1959 to connect the freight terminal with Tinsley marshalling yard. To compensate, the next lock, just beyond the new bridge, was rebuilt with a larger drop in level; note the metal casing for the huge paddle gearing. Consequently the twelve locks have become eleven, grouped as four (behind) and seven (ahead). At the next there is an old milepost marking the first mile since leaving the river, and an electrified railway, the Manchester line via Woodhead Tunnel, comes alongside to the left. A second railway to the right joins the canal at the next lock; note the stone block in the chamber bearing the legend 'Blitzed Dec. 15

1940', a reminder of World War II air raids on the city. Two locks further on, a high-level footbridge crosses the chamber giving access to buses and pubs at Attercliffe Common. Views open up as the locks are climbed with Wincobank hill fort again in view, this time to the right. The penultimate lock is accompanied by a scrapyard, whilst the top one shows some impressive earthworks supporting the chamber and the channel.

If you wish to sample water travel, a waterbus runs on summer Sundays between the head of the locks and Sheffield Basin (details from Aubrey Green's boatyard, Sheffield 731713). There are two intermediate stops, at Worksop Road and Staniforth Road. Note the remains of a bascule railway bridge which once served Tinsley Park Colliery, before crossing to the left of the canal at the first road bridge. The name Broughton Lane commemorates Spence Broughton, a highwayman hanged here in 1791, whilst to the south a half-mile branch once followed the line of Greenland Road to a colliery pumping engine. Beyond the bridge the towpath becomes enclosed by a high brick wall and can be muddy. The railway still accompanies the canal, soon crossed by an ugly brick-and-steel bridge and overshadowed by the huge Morton Steels plant to the right.

Soon you reach Darnall Aqueduct. A listed structure, it is built of masonry with three arches. The large central arch carries the roadway flanked by smaller arches carrying footpaths at a higher level. Beyond it the canal bends right; geese and ducks share possession of this section. Here the railway leaves the canal, and there is access to Shirland Road together with several benches for the foot-weary walker.

Two high-level concrete bridges on stilts mark the entry to Attercliffe cutting, 150yd long and up to 36ft deep. The cutting has a forlorn look with rubbish strewn about its sides. At its far end the bridge carrying the A57 gives access to Staniforth Road. There are more benches, and a view opens ahead of Quarry Bank Flats. Milepost 3 is passed before Bacon Lane Bridge is reached, a handsome original masonry arch with a brick parapet. Beyond it two houseboats are moored, the first sign of navigable life. The canal is now very enclosed; further concrete and steel bridges cross it. The next arch bridge is a fine brick structure built on the skew. Note the wall on the opposite side; it is topped with halves of old grindstones and is partly made from 'crozzle', a rough black material made of dust from grindstones mixed with sand and used as a seal in cementation furnaces.

At a wide brick arched railway bridge the towpath is blocked. Turning left through a doorway brings you on to Blast Lane. Turning right it is a quarter of a mile to the canal terminus. Suddenly you have left the eighteenth- and nineteenth-century waterway world and been thrust back into the dangerous mêlée of twentieth-century motorways. The basin is situated by a huge roundabout marking the end of the Parkway, a dual carriageway link with the M1. High level footbridges take you over the traffic to the railway station a quarter of a mile away, but if you have time it is worth exploring the canal terminus. Through an archway in a cobbled yard is a fine curved terrace, with office buildings dating from the 1850s together with the original 1819 warehouse. A later warehouse dating from 1896 and built of concrete straddles the basin; once it enabled boats to unload through trapdoors under shelter. Although the basin has been blighted for many years, plans have been agreed for a development scheme which involves converting the two ware-houses for recreational and catering use, building a hotel, and resurfacing and relighting the basin surround. A new towpath bridge will provide access to the basin from the canal and the intention is to retain the 'working canal' atmosphere as far as possible.

For more information about the Tinsley to Sheffield section, the City Museums publish a guide *Navigation: the story of the Sheffield and Tinsley Canal.*

17 THE STAFFORDSHIRE & WORCESTERSHIRE CANAL ·
Simon Ross *Stourton to Cookley (5 miles)*

Almost the entire length of the Staffordshire & Worcestershire Canal has been declared a conservation area, so protecting it from any unplanned development. You can soon see why, as you walk the stretch from Stourton to Cookley. The Staffordshire & Worcestershire meanders alongside the River Stour through some of the most attractive scenery in the two counties. Contrasting with the scenic beauty and adding to the character of the canal are the relics of the economic past. Long before the canal was opened in 1772, the River Stour, which had been made navigable in parts, was of significant importance in the early days of the Industrial Revolution as iron was smelted at a number of riverside sites. The opening of the canal led to the expansion of existing industries and the creation of new ones.

The Staffordshire & Worcestershire, nearly 46 miles in length, connects the Trent & Mersey Canal at Great Haywood with the River Severn at Stourport. The Stourton to Cookley walk is about five miles long, without taking any of the many possible detours, and the condition of the towpath is generally good. Join the towpath at Stewponey Lock, accessible along a path opposite a layby on the A458 to the south of Stourton near the A449 crossroads. It is worth walking northwards above the lock for 200 yards to Stourton Junction, where the Stourbridge Canal joins the Staffordshire and Worcestershire. The Stourbridge Canal, opened in 1779, provided a link with the industrial Black Country and this junction, now so peaceful and encircled by trees and hedges, was extremely busy in the days of the working boats. There is a fine view from the towpath bridge of the Stourbridge Canal, looking south. To the right is the River Stour, never far away on your walk. Beyond the field to the right is the impressive Stourton Castle, where a local parliamentary leader, Colonel 'Tinker' Fox, planted a garrison during the Civil War. In the castle grounds there used to be an ancient ironworks, although today, as with most of the old ironworks in the valley, nothing remains. Straight ahead in the

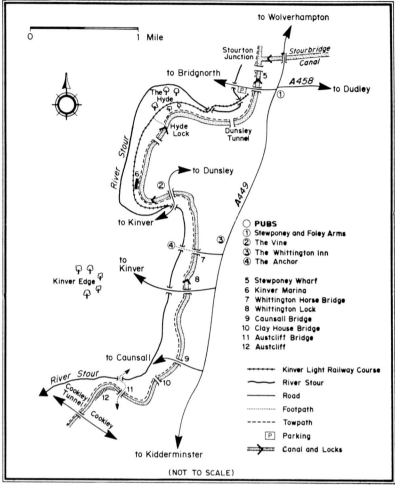

Map 11 The Staffordshire & Worcestershire Canal: Stourton to Cookley

distance is the village of Kinver with, on the skyline, the up-standing wooded Kinver Edge.

Return to Stewponey Lock and examine the buildings on the wharf. The toll-house close to the lock is reputed to have been one of the busiest on the canal; as late as the early 1930s records show over eight hundred loaded boats passing here in a six-month period. The row of buildings behind the toll-house incorporates a lock-keeper's cottage on the far left and, adjoining it, converted stables. The British Waterways Board is converting these buildings into a maintenance depot. To the right of the stables is a canal-worker's cottage.

An interesting story relates to the pub you can see beyond the buildings and to the name Stewponey. It is said to be derived from the Spanish town of Estepona, the home town of the bride of one of Wellington's soldiers in the Peninsular War. The soldier brought his wife to England and opened an inn, naming it after her home town, more or less. Whatever the truth of this, there used to be a pub by the main road crossroads, near the site of the present Stewponey and Foley Arms. The earlier house was demolished in the 1930s; its successor offers a grill room as well as the usual facilities. The green at the side is the scene of Baring Gould's novel *Bladys of the Stewponey*.

Walk from the lock beneath the two bridges, Old Stewponey Bridge, number 32, and the modern road bridge, number 31A. There is a towpath underpass beneath the first, a relatively unusual feature. Here there used to be a trestle bridge that carried the Kinver Light Railway, the course of which you will see later in the walk. The railway was built at the end of the nineteenth century by the British Electric Traction Co and was opened in 1901. The track, 3ft 6in gauge, ran alongside the Stourbridge–Stewponey road, crossing the canal near Bridge 32 and thence running alongside the canal to Kinver. It linked the Black Country, Colbournbrook and Amblecote, with Kinver village but succumbed to road competition and was closed in 1930. Continuing towards Dursley Tunnel, note the varied flora typical of lowland waterside environments. Mostly the stretch is tree- and hedge-lined, with weeping willow, hawthorn and elderberry much in evidence. See also several varieties of thistle and parsley, with foxglove, balsam, great and rosebay willow herb and vetch. Look out for the control paddle gear to a run-off weir to the River Stour; there are several of these along the route.

Soon the canal curves to the right and narrows to enter Dursley Tunnel, only 23ft long, carved out of the New Red Sandstone and unlined except for some brick reinforcement at the northern end. Unusually, the towpath continues through it. Inside the tunnel note the grooves made by the ropes of the horse-drawn boats and the multicoloured evidence of the collisions of pleasure craft with the tunnel sides. The sandstone contains many pebbles and is an exposure of the Bunter Pebble Beds, gravelly deposits laid down over 200 million years ago by huge rivers flowing northwards over the Triassic desert environment. Beyond the tunnel are several brick pillars in the sandstone, inserted to prevent the collapse of overhanging rock.

As you walk on, notice the sudden increase of woodland to your right. This area is known as The Hyde. It is private, but look over the fence and you will see marked undulations, about the only remaining visible evidence of the Hyde Ironworks, the largest and one of the oldest of the canalside ironworks with twenty puddling furnaces and many mills and forges. Like most of the other ironworks, it predates the canal, although it grew rapidly with the improved supplies of canal-borne iron from the Black Country. In the late 1800s the works had a canal frontage of some 400ft and its own private branch, now disappeared. In the 1880s, however, the works closed; almost all the buildings have since vanished and the slag heaps were used for ballast. A modernised whitewashed house just before the next lock is reputed to be the last remains of the Hyde complex. The course of the light railway can be discerned about twenty yards along a path leading into the woods nearby. Hyde Lock has a lockkeeper's cottage, with a sandstone exposure, the Dune Sands, to the side of it. This is a desert dune formation, laid down before the Bunter Pebble Beds and the oldest rock exposure along the walk. Beyond the lock and bridge to the right you can see two pipes crossing the Stour, replacing the bridges that used to carry the Kinver Light Railway and the footpath that succeeded it.

Now you are nearing Kinver, with predominantly private moorings lining the towpath and Kinver Marina to the right. Straight ahead on the horizon is the wooded rise called Kinver Edge, upstanding as the underlying Dune Sands are protected by the more resistant Pebble Beds. Kinver Pumping Station, just past the marina, raises water from the Dune Sands. It is built on the site of the light railway terminus; you may be able to discern traces of the route. Then you come to Kinver Lock and bridge, with The Vine close by, where sandwiches or more substantial meals may be obtained. For the village, turn right at the lock, passing the famous sandstone caves supposedly once inhabited by boatmen and their families, and after a short uphill walk you arrive at St Peter's Church, which dates from the Saxon period and dominates the village. Kinfare, as the village's name used to be spelled and still is on the canal bridge, derives from Kine-fair, an old cattle market, although there are few cattle in evidence today.

Returning to the towpath note how the left bank dips steeply down to the canal and how lush the gardens are. You will see horse chestnut and oaks here, as well as exposures of sandstone illustrating the geological phenomenon of cross-bedding. Soon the woodland yields to pasture and willow herb again becomes prolific. Whittington Horse Bridge is the next you come to. This was originally built to take horses carrying iron across the canal to a local ironworks but was not used for long as wharves were soon constructed as the traffic increased. These, now privately owned, can still be seen near the bridge. Two interesting pubs are nearby. The Whittington Inn on the A449, accessible along a lane between the cottages over the bridge, was once a manor house belonging to Dick Whittington's grandfather and an inn since the late eighteenth century. The second pub, The Anchor, can be reached along a path from the bridge but heading in the opposite direction and crossing the Stour. The path crosses the site of another ironworks, and The Anchor, dating from the fifteenth century, was connected with the works; nailers' cottages make up part of its premises.

Back on the towpath you soon pass Old Mill Cottage, whose pond was associated with the ironworks, and then arrive at Whittington Lock and bridge. You may rest on a bench dedicated to the memory of Jim Robbins, chairman of the Staffordshire & Worcestershire Canal Society 1964–67. To regain the towpath you have to cross the road; thence you pass through an avenue of trees, the path being overgrown in spring and summer, with tufted vetch, meadowsweet and deadly nightshade being common. After fighting your way through the butterbur, in about half a mile you reach Caunsall Bridge, with large sandstone blocks indicating the line of the original arch. The road to the right leads to Caunsall village.

Two hundred yards further on, in attractive open countryside, is Clay House Bridge, an official ancient monument and one of the finest surviving Brindley accommodation bridges.

Then comes Austcliff Bridge, with perhaps the best-known natural feature on the canal beyond it: Austcliff, an impressive sandstone cliff 25ft high, awesomely overhanging the waterway. It is the proximity of the Stour that forced the canal up against the sandstone; the alternative would have required a tunnel or a series of aqueducts, both expensive. Austcliff is a further exposure of the Bunter Pebble Beds, which explains why it is abruptly upstanding. Cross-bedding is again visible in the sandstone. Two pubs, The Anchor and The Rock Tavern, can be reached by crossing the footbridge over the Stour and following the path to Caunsall.

Now you are nearing the end of the walk. Gradually you become aware of the canal narrowing and actually seeming to disappear ahead beneath a row of terraced houses. It is about to enter Cookley Tunnel, which passes right underneath the main street of Cookley and has wharves at either end. This is the oldest tunnel on the entire waterway system and the longest on the Staffordshire & Worcestershire, stretching for all of 65yd. As at Dursley, the towpath is carried through.

Cookley itself grew up as an iron-making village centred on a seventeenth-century ironworks. This declined and was moved in 1886 to Brierley Hill. In its place a steel stampings works was set up, which used water-borne transport until the 1930s. The works can be seen just beyond the tunnel and form a fitting end to the walk as a modern reminder of the industrial past of the Stour valley with its river and canal. The iron bridge fifty yards on from the tunnel crosses the line of an old canal arm. A path beyond the tunnel leads to Cookley High Street.

18 THE STROUDWATER CANAL ·
Michael Handford
Framilode to Wallbridge (7 miles)

The best way to reach the small riverside hamlet of Framilode is to catch the regular Swanbrook service from Gloucester bus station. Take the road on the Frome left bank facing downstream. The long gardens of Canal Row on your left were probably a navvy encampment in 1775–6 when the canal was started. The black-and-white former New Inn on your right, originally a boatmen's tavern, was later a grace-and-favour house owned by the canal company. The former lock-house and warehouse stand beyond this facing the basin site and infilled river lock.

Walk up the towpath behind Canal Row noticing the large bricks which suggest that the houses were built soon after the canal was opened in 1779. This area, known as Carters Close, was the site of a famous skirmish between canal supporters and opponents. There were several pubs along here but only The Ship Inn now remains. You can buy *A Towpath Guide to the Stroudwater, Thames & Severn Canals,* and take refreshment here. Approaching Moor Street Bridge you pass the former Cookley's Wharf and stable. Where the canal and river have been amalgamated in a flood relief scheme, follow the right-hand bank for about half a mile, pass the old Drum and Monkey pub and, keeping to the left-hand side of the boat-house, you then emerge onto the Gloucester & Berkeley Canal towpath.

Saul Junction is an interesting area. The route of the Kemmett Canal followed the line of the Frome behind Junction Bridge House. The ship canal, built to avoid the dangerous Severn tides, reached here from Gloucester in 1820. To meet on a level, the pound of the Stroudwater from here to Whitminster Lock was raised to the Berkeley level and a new lock, Junction Lock, installed. Built and maintained by the Gloucester & Berkeley Canal Company the design of the gates, type of balance beam, style of paddle gear, lock-bridge and building materials all mark it out as different from the usual Stroudwater pattern. The iron swing bridge across the Stroudwater Canal

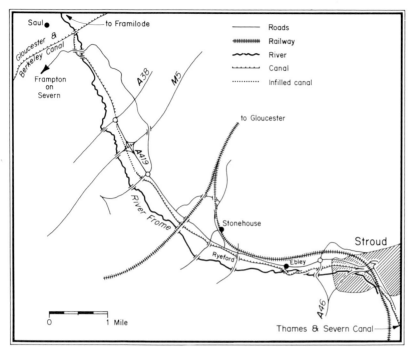

Map 12 The Stroudwater Canal

entrance opposite was installed about 1886, replacing an earlier wooden one. Others put in then included those at Framilode, Ryeford, Ebley Cloth Mills and near Stroud Gas Works. Drop into the office at Junction Bridge House where Harold Brown, the friendly bridge-keeper, provides tea and sandwiches in his garden or cosy office according to season. You can see the line of the earlier Cambridge (c.1750) and Kemmett (1759–63) canals following the Frome line in his garden. The private Cambridge Canal was built by Richard Owen Cambridge from Framilode to Bristol Road to improve his Whitminster estate. The unique container canal built by John Kemmett from Framilode to Stonehouse had cranes instead of locks to effect the change in level. The pre-1820 Stroudwater Canal ran halfway between the river and the house.

Follow the towpath past the small pleasure boathouse on the offside and up the embanked post-1820 Stroudwater Canal here built on the route of the original 1775–79 canal as well. Cross

115

the road carefully at Walk Bridge and continue to the site of Whitminster Lock. The fall was reduced from about 4ft to a few inches when the canal was raised to join the Berkeley Canal level. The towpath crosses to the right-hand bank here where canal and river have both been incorporated into a flood relief scheme. Walk through or round the wood, over the double stile, over the river footbridge and rejoin the canal on your left. The river, to your right, formed the earlier Cambridge and Kemmett canals line.

Notice the war-time pillboxes on this pound and the dredging mounds on the right of the towpath. The fixed Stonepits Bridge, named from nearby gravel workings, precedes the well-preserved Occupation Bridge characteristic of the canal in the Vale of Gloucester where building materials used reflect the underlying clay geology. The similarity to some Midland canal bridges confirms both the simple utility of the design and the way engineers and clerks of works moved from one canal to

Bow-hauling on the Stroudwater Canal by Stonehouse Church, 1781 *(drawn and engraved by T. Bonner)*

another using the same basic patterns of construction with local variations. Stroudwater links with the Staffordshire & Worcestershire Canal and Droitwich Barge Canal are especially strong. There are some striking examples of rope markings beneath the bridge and a good view of the Cambridge and Kemmett canals across the valley. This quiet attractive stretch is superbly maintained by Tuffley Angling Club.

The canal was opened to Bristol Road Wharf in December 1776, and the two houses here were occupied by company clerks and later by managers. The canal is blocked here, so follow the road opposite built on the canal line turning right at the next island to Chippenham Platt. Looking down the canal, you can see the wharf on your right with its Georgian wharf-house similar to others along the canal. The remains of Court Orchard or Dock Lock are visible further down. The canal maintenance yard with a manager's house still standing, carpenter's shop, blacksmith's shop and dry dock stood on the offside here.

Look upstream to Pike Lock and the Victorian replacement lock-house. From here the canal runs through an attractive wooded stretch to Blunder and Nassfield locks. There is some circumstantial evidence suggesting that the resident engineer, Edmund Lingard, already under a month's notice, deliberately planned the former lock on the wrong level to teach a persistently interfering committee of directors a lesson they would never forget. The popularly dubbed Blunder Lock was rebuilt soon afterwards using local stone. There is an interesting overflow weir above the lock. Nassfield Lock is a standard brick chamber with local limestone capping. The small hamlet of Newtown is a 'new town' created as a navvies' encampment and later a canalside settlement including pub and boatmen's cottages. Notice again the very long gardens on the other side of the road.

Roving Bridge carries the towpath back to the downside bank. Stone foundations protrude slightly at water level to keep trows, Stroudwater barges, and long boats away from the structure. There are large dredging mounds on the towpath side. Originally a woollen mill, Bonds Mill used coal delivered by canal. Boats rested a plank on the gunwales with the other end on a cart positioned between the two iron gates. Boatmen then used shovels to fill wheelbarrows from the boat, ran them along the plank and tipped them into the cart.

For the next mile the canal is built along the edge of the spur with a steep drop to the valley below. John Kemmett's canal ran parallel at the bottom of the towpath bank; the River Frome now uses this course as one of its channels. Hoffman's Weir supplies water to a factory nearby, but it will be superfluous when the canal is restored to its former level.

The original towpath along the full length of the canal was narrower than the present one. Until 1825, when both the Gloucester & Berkeley and the Thames & Severn Canal Companies persuaded the owners to install a horse towpath, man towage on a narrow towpath unsuitable for animals was the norm. This was unusual on artificial navigations but logical for a branch canal from the Severn which itself had no towing path for animals at the time.

Stonehouse Ocean is an attractive waterspace enhanced by its traditional swans. It was always a popular overnight mooring spot for generations of local day boatmen who walked or, in later years, cycled home from here. Stonehouse Court Hotel is ideal for a brief rest. Take the door through the stone wall near the church and enter through the back door; you can buy good country food in the bar. Ocean Swing Bridge has sandstone copings from Gatcombe on the River Wye and Cotswold limestone copings from nearby Rodborough Hill. St Cyr's Church lost part of its churchyard when the canal was constructed. John Kemmett's canal in the valley below was abandoned when it reached this point.

Nutshell Cottage, House and Bridge are something of an enigma. Clearly all built at the same time, they suggest 'look out' residences for the company. Nevertheless there is no evidence that they ever belonged to the company nor is there any reason why the company required such a facility here. A coal pen by Nutshell House for Stanley Mill is an inadequate answer. Stonehouse Wharf near the demolished Bridgend Bridge was the second largest wharf. The wharf-house still stands but is threatened with demolition by a road scheme. The Ship Inn on the offside bank has forgotten its earlier links. Until recently its inn sign showed a large sea-going vessel. Near Upper Mill swing bridge Wycliffe College boathouse now stands disused. The new boathouse is at Saul Junction.

Near Ryeford Bridge there are two coal pens for Stanley and Ryeford mills. The former Anchor Inn, now a private house, and Ryeford Wharf are on the offside. The bridge has been extended towards Stroud. The towpath underneath was only wide enough for man haulage so after 1825 mules went over the road instead of underneath. The cottages opposite the former Ryeford Corn Mills were probably built for boatmen and canal workers. From here the towpath runs on a narrow ledge between the canal and River Frome as far as the impressive Ryeford Double Locks designed by Anthony Keck; they cost £760, a considerable sum by the standards of the time. Notice the massive stone copings. The company-built lock-house is similar to other houses at Framilode, Bristol Road and Chippenham Platt. The circular trunks were installed to drain nearby land, reducing water pressure after the locks collapsed late in 1779. The two top pounds to Wallbridge were built deeper than the rest of the canal to act as reservoirs of 'Sunday water' not needed by the local mills. The warehouse standing at right angles to the canal on Ebley Saw Mills Wharf was probably built by the canal company. Nearly opposite, an unusual circular weir carried surplus water from the canal. There is another circular weir just past Bell Bridge.

Follow the canal through the former Ebley Cloth Mills to the Hilly Orchard footbridge. From here to Dudbridge Locks the towpath is only passable with difficulty so you can turn right at Hilly Orchard then left and out onto the main road as far as the locks. If you follow the towpath, notice the large listed stone-built property called Gladfield Gardens on your right. This was owned by Wards, the coal merchants, for many years when they operated from Dudbridge Wharf which lies between the house and the bridge. There is an iron rubbing straight beneath the bridge and an iron hook for boats waiting for the lock. The keystone on the Stroud side is dated 1778. Dudbridge Locks were built by William Franklin, a stonemason, in 1778–79. The houses on the offside were reputedly cider houses for boatmen. At the Upper Lock the stonework has been shaped skilfully to take the gate paddle. The last cargo of ten tons of coal was unloaded at Stroud Gas Works Wharf in 1941 across the blue edging bricks. Dudbridge Coal Wharf was on the offside beyond Gas Works Bridge in front of the stone house.

The towpath now swings to the right with the Lodgemore Mills millpond on the offside. The Painswick Stream acts as a feeder further on. The rough land opposite Lodgemore Mills was originally the site of Benjamin Grazebrook's luxurious home, Far Hill, built on the profits of the canal and the carrying trade. Beyond Lodgemore Mills the land between the canal and the river formed a large wharf. This is Wallbridge, the canal port of Stroud. The Thames & Severn Canal leaves the Stroudwater Canal here and runs behind the 1779 company warehouse and the Georgian canal company headquarters built in 1795–97. Wallbridge Basin, the terminus of the Stroudwater Canal, was infilled in 1954.

19 THE WORCESTER & BIRMINGHAM CANAL · Simon Ross

Hanbury Wharf to Stoke Pound (4½ miles)

The Worcester & Birmingham Canal provides the shortest water link between the industrial West Midlands and the Westcountry via the River Severn. This explains its importance as a trading route, although it was never as successful as the nearby Staffordshire & Worcestershire. It stimulated much economic growth along its length, some of which can be seen today in varying states of decay and redevelopment. Moreover, it passes through attractive Worcestershire countryside and close to several interesting villages.

The Worcester & Birmingham was authorised by Act of Parliament in 1791 but it was not completed until 1815. The climb to the Birmingham plateau made construction difficult; in its 30 miles there had to be 108 locks and a long tunnel. The delays cost the canal company dearly as it was unable to trade in the busy years of the early nineteenth century. Commercial traffic ended some years ago but the canal is in reasonably good condition and popular for pleasure cruising.

The walk, 4½ miles long, begins at Hanbury Wharf on the B4090, two miles east of Droitwich and on a local bus route. This is a Roman road and is still known as the Salt Way. Droitwich was a salt town in Roman times and local prosperity stemmed from the salt industry. Hanbury Wharf is now the home of Ladyline boat builders. The buildings by the road were associated with the economic life of the canal and the small building beside the towpath was a stables. Obvious is a tall white feature resembling a lighthouse, the iron tree of a ten-ton crane that used to operate on the wharf. Obvious also is The Eagle and Sun pub where you can take refreshment before beginning the walk.

Having gained the towpath, head northwards. Across the canal look for the entrance to the disused Droitwich Junction Canal which the Droitwich Canal Trust hopes eventually to reopen. It runs parallel to the Salt Way and descends through seven narrow locks to join the abandoned Droitwich Canal, now

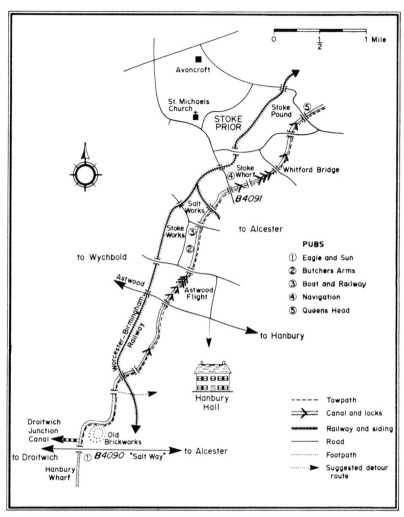

Map 13 The Worcester & Birmingham Canal: Hanbury to Stoke Pound

being actively restored. In about a hundred yards you will see on your right a considerable amount of infilling and landscaping taking place. This is the site of the Hanbury Wharf Brickworks which used the canal for transport until World War I. To your left beyond the pasture land you can see the line of the M5 motorway and the transmitters at nearby Wychbold.

Flora and fauna are varied along the walk. Hedgerows

dominate the canal banks and there are many different flowers to see including meadowsweet, various willow herbs and parsleys and the occasional rarer wild flowers. Butterflies and dragonflies are common in the summer.

Approaching Bridge 36 note the main Worcester–Birmingham railway line to your right. The small hill on the right is Summer Hill. A few yards before the bridge look for a gap in the hedge through which you can gain access to the bridge and enjoy good views of the surrounding countryside. A footpath heading east will take you to Hanbury Hall, a red brick house in the Wren style built in 1701 and owned by the National Trust; check opening times first if you want to visit (you can phone the Hall direct on 052 784214).

Bridge 37, made of large sandstone blocks exhibiting the honeycomb effect of weathering, takes the railway across the canal. The next section, through Bridge 38, is especially attractive with vigorous hedges and a wide variety of flora. As you round a gentle curve to the left you will see the familiar black and white of a lock standing out clearly against the green surround. Look out for the steel supports across the towpath, forming part of the bank defences. The absence of a bridge adds to the remote quietness of this lock. Until recently there was a lock-keeper's cottage, built at the same time as the Droitwich Junction to take tolls on the traffic between Birmingham and Droitwich. Now only the remains of a brick wall to the right of the top gate give visual evidence of its existence.

A few hundred yards further on, narrowing of the canal denotes the site of a recently demolished accommodation bridge. Between here and Bridge 40 look out for kingfishers as this stretch is renowned for them. To the left of Bridge 40 is the hamlet of Astwood, which gives its name to the flight of five locks you are now approaching. By the first lock is a lock-keeper's cottage where you may buy tea or coffee. The next lock stands isolated in open countryside and the remaining three are close together with only short passing pounds between them. From the top lock, number 22, you can see Wychbold Church on the skyline to your left.

At Bridge 41 you enter a more industrialised section of canal. You are approaching the dispersed settlement of Stoke, comprising Stoke Prior, Stoke Works, Stoke Wharf and Stoke

The Tardebigge flight of locks on the Worcester & Birmingham Canal
(British Waterways Board)

Pound. Salt was obtained here from brine pumped up from the underlying rocks, and remnants of the industry can be seen alongside the canal, once its transport lifeline. Stoke Works village lies on the left with a couple of older houses visible among the modern dwellings. The Butchers Arms and shops are accessible from Bridge 42, and the block of buildings by the bridge includes an old boatmen's tavern, The Boat and Railway, and a converted stables. On the further side of the bridge are the demolished buildings of the salt works, knocked down in the 1970s and awaiting redevelopment. These works, built by John Corbett after brine was discovered here in 1828, were reputed to be 'the most complete and compact in the world'. Corbett built workers' houses, known locally as 'Salty Homes' alongside the works, paid £4,500 to restore Stoke Prior Church and also paid for a school to be built. He was MP for Droitwich and built the imposing Chateau Impney near Droitwich to please his homesick French wife. Although he is buried in Stoke Prior churchyard, it is said that you may see him occasionally riding his white horse through the village streets.

The sweet, rubbery smell you may become aware of emanates from the synthetic rubber factory of Bayer UK, which also now owns the site of the old salt works. Continue through the fumes; soon the towpath lifts across the entrance to a disused arm of the canal. Beyond the railway bridge there used to be a boatyard where in 1906 George Farrin built the first motor-propelled commercial boat on this canal. Approaching Bridge 44 you pass one of Stoke's many small factories. The bridge carries the Stoke–Hanbury road, the B4091; some fifty yards along to the left is The Navigation, a pub which serves food and has a beer garden.

Through the bridge on the left is Stoke Wharf, once very busy with a weighbridge, two coal merchants, a hay, straw and corn merchant and various warehouses. Black Prince Narrow-boats now own the wharf and their hirers can turn their boats at the winding point nearby.

Between Bridges 45 and 46 you are back in the countryside again with weeds, rushes and lilies lining the water and many wild flowers by the towpath. You pass three locks, set close together. Bridge 46, Whitford Bridge, has a row of old canal cottages beside it. Beyond this bridge the view opens out. To your left you can see a windmill, part of Avoncroft Museum. Carry on along the towpath (this area is Stoke Pound) and past Lock 28 to Bridge 48 and The Queen's Head, a large, well-equipped pub where you can refresh yourself and enjoy a meal before retracing your steps to Hanbury Wharf.

If you have time, however, it is well worth leaving the canal at this point and diverting to visit the Avoncroft Museum and Stoke Prior Church. Turn left on to the road at the bridge, walk past The Queen's Head and continue for about a mile. At the summit of a slight hill you arrive at the museum. This is an open-air museum of historic buildings and includes a fifteenth-century merchant's house, a chain-making workshop, a barn, granary and post mill. It occupies a ten-acre site and is open from the beginning of March to the end of November.

From the museum return down the hill, take a right turn and

follow the pretty country lane to St Michael's Church. The tower dates from the thirteenth century but much of the building was restored with John Corbett's money. To rejoin the canal turn left at the lychgate and walk straight on for about 1½ miles until you reach Stoke Wharf.

You may, of course, continue into Birmingham along the towpath, a distance of just over 16 miles from The Queen's Head to Gas Street Basin. Certainly if time permits it is worth continuing for a further 2¾ miles, ascending by the Tardebigge flight of thirty locks to Bridge 56 carrying the A448 across the canal and from where you can catch a bus to either Redditch or Bromsgrove.

20 THE KENNET & AVON CANAL ·
Ronald Russell
Reading to Bath (86½ miles)

The Kennet & Avon is a major element in a broad east–west
waterway route across the southern half of England, a route of
one hundred miles from the River Kennet's junction with the
Thames to the Severn estuary at Avonmouth. The canal itself is
86½ miles long, with 106 locks. It was opened throughout in
1810 and traded profitably until the opening of the Great
Western main line railway from London to Bristol in 1841. The
Great Western Railway bought the canal a few years later and
made some effort to run it properly; after a time, however,
enthusiasm waned, losses accrued and the condition of the canal
deteriorated rapidly. Efforts by the railway to close the canal
were defeated by local authorities, landowners and traders, and
a little traffic, both commercial and pleasure, struggled on.
Soon after rail and canal transport were nationalised in 1948
further attempts to close the waterway were made, this time by
the British Transport Commission. The Kennet & Avon, however, was fortunate in attracting a strong and vocal body of
voluntary supporters, which has now become the Kennet &
Avon Canal Trust. The Trust, together with the British Waterways Board who are fully aware of the value of this splendid
waterway, is leading the work of restoration. Much of the canal
is once again navigable, and it will not be many years before the
final lock is restored and through navigation becomes a reality.

The towpath of the Kennet & Avon is walkable throughout.
There are several guides to sections of its length, but the indispensable guide to the full walk is Kenneth Clew's *Wessex
Waterway* which slips easily into the pocket. Valuable also are
the two charts of the canal by Nicholas Hammond, published
by Imray, Laurie, Norie & Wilson Ltd. The brief description
that follows owes much to Kenneth Clew's book and is intended
to give no more than an idea of the distances and principal
features of this fascinating route.

You join the towpath in Reading; there are several bridges
and no difficulties of access apart from the short stretch between

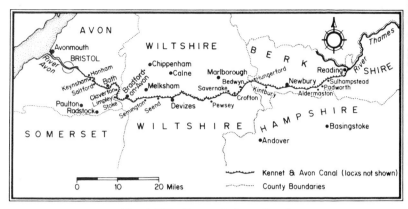

Map 14 The Kennet & Avon Canal

High Bridge and Bridge Street Bridge, known as Brewery Gut after the adjacent Courage Brewery. County Lock is the first you come to; from here in the summer you can enjoy a boat trip or picnic in the recently landscaped surrounds. Stepping around the anglers, you now head through suburban Reading and into the countryside. The waterway here is a canalisation of the River Kennet and you will note the fast-flowing river leaving and re-entering the navigation from time to time. It is a mile from County Lock to Fobney Lock and a further mile to Southcote Lock; pumping stations by these two locks provide most of Reading's water. Another mile brings you to Burghfield village which has a wharf, and a pub, The Cunning Man, for refreshment; there are osier beds on the far side of the substantial bridge.

Most of the next series of locks were originally turf-sided, being built of timber to the lower water level with sloping turf sides above, fenders being installed to keep boats off. Many have been rebuilt or replaced. At Burghfield a new lock was constructed a few yards above the turf-sided one and was opened by Sir Frank Price, chairman of the British Waterways Board, in 1968. Garston Lock, on the far side of the M4 embankment, and Sheffield Lock, three-quarters of a mile further on, are both working examples of turf-sided locks, while at Sulhamstead, in a notably beautiful setting, the present lock was constructed inside the confines of the original one, much of the work being done by prisoners from Oxford gaol. The next

128

lock, Tyle Mill, has also been restored and was reopened, together with Towney Lock 1½ miles along, in 1976. The shallow-rise Ufton Lock, in between them, is no longer in use.

So far you have been walking alongside a navigable waterway, properly called the Kennet Navigation. This navigation continues into Newbury but the remaining eight miles are unusable by boats as the locks still await restoration. Examine the remains of the old locks, note the achievements of the voluntary working parties and speculate on the cost—in cash and effort—of completing the task. Work on Padworth Lock, first on the derelict section, is in progress and it is hoped that a start will be made at Aldermaston Lock in 1983. On the question of cost, more than £95,600 was spent on restoration work during 1981. The old turf locks sadly cannot be restored but have to be rebuilt completely, according to the British Waterways Board's requirements, and one of these will cost about the same as was raised in 1981 for the whole waterway.

On this length the canal tends to avoid the villages: Theale and Sulhamstead are each about half a mile from the towpath and Aldermaston is nearly 1½ miles to the south. Woolhampton, nearly two miles on from Aldermaston Wharf, is closer at hand and The Row Barge Inn is accessible from the swing bridge, one of many you will come across. To the north, pleasant wooded countryside stretches away, gently rising.

In the six miles between Woolhampton and Newbury there are seven more locks. Heal's Lock is turf-sided but the next, Midgham, was rebuilt in brick by the Great Western Railway. Then you approach the large industrial site of Colthrop Mill, where paper has been manufactured for over a hundred and seventy years. Colthrop Lock is in the middle of the site. If you left Reading in the morning and do not feel you can reach Newbury for the night, leave the towpath at the next bridge and turn right for Thatcham a mile away where there is a good inn, The King's Head, in the market place.

Two more derelict turf-sided locks, Monkey Marsh and Widmead, are separated by a straight three-quarter mile stretch, with Thatcham marshes on either side. The Kennet, which has been straggling away to the south of your walk, rejoins the canal after Widmead Lock and leaves again by Bull's Lock, this one rebuilt in 1976 by the Canal Trust. Newbury Racecourse now appears on your left. Soon come Ham Mills Lock, recently rebuilt, and in another mile Greenham Lock, rebuilt in 1972. Now, near the centre of Newbury, you are approaching the end of the Kennet Navigation. The car park on the far side of the modern skew road bridge has obliterated the navigation's Newbury Wharf. Apart from a granary, the only remaining old building was originally stabling; this is now used by the Canal Trust. On the edge of the wharf area is an inn, The Rising Sun. If you have walked the whole length of the Kennet Navigation from the junction with the Thames you have now covered $18\frac{1}{2}$ miles; subtract half a mile if you began at County Lock.

To explore the area properly you need a little booklet called *The Canal at Newbury,* written by L. J. Dalby and published by the Canal Trust. Like most other market towns Newbury has suffered from the architects and developers of the mid-twentieth century, but not excessively so; if you are not in a hurry it is worth spending a couple of hours simply strolling around and looking. The canalside is one of the more interesting areas. The towpath takes you to, but not under, Newbury Bridge, built about 1770 before construction of the canal towards Bath had begun. There being no provision for a towpath, the walker has to cross Northbrook Street and return through a passage beside W. H. Smith's. Horses were forbidden to tow across the street, so a long line was attached to a float and sent down to the waiting barge while the horse crossed the road; then the horse was attached to the other end of the line and began pulling. The float and other evidence can be seen on the wall of the lock-cottage at Newbury Lock, a short distance above the bridge. The lock itself, with its ground paddles operated by levers, is said to be unique; it was the first to be built on the canal. Above the lock Town and West Mills used to dominate the scene; both have disappeared but the buildings on the West Mill site harmonise with the canal surroundings. The Watermill Theatre, on the banks of the River Lambourn, is about one and a half miles from Newbury Lock and well worth a visit if you are staying in Newbury overnight. You may also hire a boat from here.

As you leave Newbury the main-line railway approaches again from the south with Guyer's and Higg's locks within the first mile and a half. From Newbury to Hungerford is 9 miles, with approximately one lock for each mile. Especially attractive are the stretch near Benham Lock, where the canal passes through an artificial lake, and Kintbury Wharf, with the comfortable Dundas Arms. In the summer the horse-drawn narrow boat *Kennet Valley* works from moorings here. This stretch of canal was reopened to navigation between 1972 and 1974. Soon the Kennet and canal part company for the last time as you enter the small market town of Hungerford, rich with memories of the Civil War, many of them centred on The Bear Hotel, an important halt on the coach route from the west to London.

Now you are on the final stretch to the summit level of the canal, with just over 7½ miles to Crofton Top Lock and twenty locks in that distance. The Duchess of Somerset's Hospital at Froxfield is worth the diversion of a few hundred yards from the towpath; it has an enormously long frontage and was originally built to accommodate a large number of widows. The chapel is open to the public. Littlecote, a Tudor mansion, is 2 miles further away.

Back on the towpath you will note that the Froxfield locks were only recently restored. Next come the locks at Little Bedwyn, where the canal bisects the village which has a wharf and an intriguing Stone Museum in Church Street, near a particularly fine church, part dating from the twelfth century, with the next lock named after it. In three-quarters of a mile you arrive at Crofton Bottom Lock, first of the steep flight of nine to the summit. Crofton Top is 34½ miles from County Lock in Reading.

In order to avoid the construction of a very long tunnel, the summit level was raised higher than originally planned and a pumping engine was installed to lift a supply from Wilton Water, through a well 40ft deep. The first Boulton & Watt beam engine, dating from 1808, was replaced by a Sims Combined engine in 1843; meanwhile a second Boulton & Watt engine had been installed in 1812. These two continued working until 1959, when they were replaced by first a diesel and then an electric pump. The Canal Trust bought the pumping station in 1968 and by the end of 1971 both engines were back in working order. They are in steam from time to time and it is worth finding out in advance whether you can make your walk coincide with the experience of seeing the world's oldest working steam-engine in action. Access to the Crofton Pumping Station is through a tunnel beneath the railway line above Lock 60. There are two other points of special interest here: one is Wilton Water, rich in birdlife, and the other the pumping station car park which adjoins a mass grave for the dead of the Battle of Bedwyn fought in 675.

The summit tunnel of the canal, Bruce (or Savernake) Tunnel, is just under a mile from Crofton Top. It is 502yd long and 17ft wide, yet despite its width there is no towpath. The canal company, always alert to the principle of noblesse oblige, named the tunnel Bruce as it was the family name of the earls of Ailesbury who had supported the canal's construction. To continue your walk, follow the path over the top of the tunnel, crossing a road near a hotel and passing beneath the railway line to rejoin the canal near the west portal. The Earl of Ailesbury built Burbage Wharf, which you soon come to, and owned Savernake Forest close by. The crane on the wharf is a replica of the original one and was made by the Army from timber given by the Crown Estates.

Very soon the summit level ends at Wootton Rivers Top Lock, first of a flight of four reopened in 1973. The pretty village of Wootton Rivers is close to the bottom lock. Here begins the Long Pound, a winding, lockless stretch to Devizes, 15 miles away. It is a fine walk through the Vale of Pewsey with hills rising steeply to the north. Pewsey Wharf is outside the little town in an attractive setting with good buildings around. In 1½ miles you come to the village of Wilcot—note the suspension bridge at Stowell Park shortly before the village—and shortly to Wilcot Wide Water, where the canal traverses the grounds of Wilcot Manor taking the form of an ornamental lake with the elaborately carved Ladies Bridge at its far end.

The towpath misses Woodborough village by half a mile but runs very close to Honey Street where the wharf used to be busy with timber and a boat-building yard. The Barge Inn, once running its own brewery, bakery, slaughterhouse and grocer's shop, was an essential part of canal life; some of its history is recorded on a plaque. Here the Canal Trust operates a paddle boat *Charlotte Dundas* in the summer.

There are several villages near the canal in the next few miles and it is worth diverting if you are interested in churches. On the approach to Devizes you will note Le Marchant Barracks, now an army museum; then you walk through a tree-lined cutting into the centre of the town. At Park Road Bridge the annual Devizes to Westminster Canoe Race begins, a very popular event first run in 1949. A new record is made almost every year, and the time is now down to about sixteen hours.

The canal helped to change the appearance of Devizes as it brought stone from Bath for houses of the early nineteenth century. Devizes was also a distributing centre for coal off the Somerset Coal Canal and its wharf was busy for many decades. It stands at the head of the most impressive flight of locks in the country, 29 in all, taking the canal down 237ft in a distance of 2 miles. Seventeen of them, known as the Caen Hill flight, seem to be stacked one on top of the other in a straight line with their side ponds stretched out beside them. They were the work of John Blackwell, superintendent engineer, and a plaque in his memory is affixed to the bridge carrying the A361 across the canal between Locks 47 and 46. In 1951 the locks were closed; rescue work began in the late 1960s and now the locks await new gates before becoming operational once more. As you descend, look for evidence of a railway that linked the upper and lower sections of canal while the locks were being completed.

From Devizes it is just over twenty miles to Bath. Two wharves named after traders on the canal, Wragg's and Scott's, follow shortly after the bottom lock; then in another mile come the five Seend locks with The Barge Inn, its sign portraying Joe Skinner's horse-drawn narrow boat *Friendship,* by the middle of the flight. The countryside is very green and fertile around here. In a further two miles come the two restored Semington locks with the blocked-up entrance to the Wiltshire & Berkshire Canal on the northern side below the bottom lock. The private house you can see used to be the toll-collector's house and there was a lock in the garden of it. You are now on the outskirts of Trowbridge, though the wharves which served the town are 2½ miles further on at Hilperton Bridge, and it is about a mile to the centre should you wish to break your journey here.

As you continue, note two aqueducts: Ladydown carries the canal over the railway and Biss across the River Biss. These are precursors of the two splendid aqueducts you are soon to reach. Before these comes Bradford on Avon, one of the route's chief

133

glories and one of England's finest small country towns. It is an ancient wool town, though much of the best building, houses of warm Cotswold stone, dates from the eighteenth century. St Lawrence's Church retains much Saxon work; Holy Trinity Church, the Town Bridge with its chantry chapel, and the enormous Tithe Barn are among the fascinations of this lovely town. Bradford rises in terraces above the Avon; the two wharves are at the centre of a small canalside settlement half a mile from the middle of the town. There is a dry dock, emptied by pulling out a plug, next to The Barge Inn. Look also for The Canal Tavern, created by knocking three cottages together, replacing the original pub of that name which is the tiny building between the towpath and the bridge.

The length between Bradford and Bath is known as the Nine Mile Pound. Much of this was drained because of the danger of landslips, and rendering it leak-proof has proved a lengthy and expensive process. In one and a half miles you arrive at the first of the two important aqueducts, the three-arch Avoncliffe Aqueduct across the river and railway. The old Crossed Guns Inn, which predates the canal by two centuries, is by the basin at Avoncliffe Wharf. There were mills on either side of the river here and the village of Westwood is three-quarters of a mile away. The aqueduct itself, about 110yd long, has been crudely repaired with brick in the past.

In this area stone was brought to the canal by tramroads from quarries in the hills; you should be able to detect the tramroad route climbing into the hills at Avoncliffe and possibly at Murhill Quarry Wharf, three-quarters of a mile from the aqueduct. The next wharf, a further mile along, is Limpley Stoke, with a fine old church and pub in the village. There are wooded slopes on your right and the river below; this is a splendid walk, its splendour increased by the Kennet & Avon's major architectural feature, the great Dundas Aqueduct, 150yd long, taking the canal back across the river and railway. This dates from the first years of the nineteenth century, being completed just after the Avoncliffe Aqueduct and also designed by John Rennie. It carries inscriptions to Charles Dundas, first chairman of the canal company, and to John Thomas, superintendent for twenty-five years. It is a masterpiece of design and masonry in Bath stone; note the elaborate balustrades and the

Dundas Aqueduct on the Kennet & Avon Canal *(from an aquatint by I. Hill after a drawing by J. C. Nattes, 1805)*

projecting cornices. Every stone carries its mason's mark. As with Avoncliffe, the east-facing side, not exposed to prevailing winds, is in better condition, although Dundas has suffered less than its neighbour from defacing repairs.

Having crossed the aqueduct, and before the canal turns right-angled to Dundas Wharf, note the cottage on your left. This was originally the lock-keeper's cottage on the Somerset Coal Canal, which joined the Kennet & Avon at this point. Much of the early prosperity of the Kennet & Avon was due to the coal traffic off the Somerset Coal Canal, and you can trace much of its course through the one-time Somerset coalfield *(see* Kenneth Clew's *The Somersetshire Coal Canal and Railways* or my *Lost Canals and Waterways of Britain,* both published by David & Charles).

There is no canalside inn at Dundas but The Viaduct Hotel is only a few yards away by the main road. A crane and warehouse survive on the wharf, where often you will meet members of the Canal Trust who will answer your questions about the progress

135

of restoration. Dundas Bridge is at the end of the wharf; then in just over a mile is the canal's second pumping station, Claverton, which lifted water from the Avon, 53ft below, in buckets operated by two water-wheels. This worked until 1952 and has been restored within the past ten years; again, you may be lucky enough to see it in action.

Bath is now near at hand. On your way are Hampton Quarry Wharf, once important for the stone trade, and the village of Bathampton where you may be able to save your feet by taking a boat trip for the remaining distance. The views on this final stretch are among the finest on the whole journey; with the steep hills around and the handsome city ahead, they are certainly the most dramatic. No canal enters a city more impressively. Darlington Old Wharf is just outside the boundary; then, instead of the usual amble through suburbs, you plunge into the 165ft tunnel of Sydney Gardens to emerge in a wooded cutting with the pleasure gardens, contemporary with the canal, above. Note the decoration on the tunnel portal and the elegant iron footbridges arching above you. You leave the gardens through a second tunnel, 173ft long, with Cleveland House, which became for many years the canal company's offices, built above it. Sydney Wharf follows shortly, with Sydney Maltings close by; then comes Bath Top Lock, with a basin below it, and six more locks of the Bath, or Widcombe, flight, leading down to the Avon. Observe especially the Deep Lock, effectively two locks in one, built in 1976 to replace a lock lost in a road improvement scheme. The reopening of the flight is commemorated by a plaque on the wall of what used to be a pumping station feeding water from the river back up the flight of locks.

In Bath, of course, there are plenty of places to stay and it is still a good inland-transport centre. Ten more miles walking alongside the Avon will bring you to Bristol and, if you want to complete one hundred miles, you can carry on to Avonmouth. But whatever you make of this final excursion, few, if any, will doubt that the Kennet & Avon from Reading to Bath provides one of the most varied and interesting long-distance walks in Britain.

21 THE LEEDS & LIVERPOOL
CANAL · Ronald Russell *(127 miles)*

Stretching across the Pennines, the Leeds & Liverpool Canal is the only remaining navigable trans-Pennine waterway route. For the long-distance cross-country walker there are more direct, and probably more exciting, ways of getting from Leeds to Liverpool, but the towpath walk takes you to places you might never otherwise dream of visiting and it can be conveniently tackled in sections taken a day or a weekend at a time.

If you want to cover the urban section of the canal, join the towpath at the bridge by Office Lock, due south of Leeds City Station. Alternatively you can save three miles by gaining the path to the west of the city near the ruins of Kirkstall Abbey, possibly after a visit to the fascinating Abbey House Museum. The canal follows the valley of the Aire, gradually ascending through a series of locks, many of them grouped in threes; for the most part you are accompanied by the railway but you avoid much of the suburban housing and industrial approaches to Leeds.

The first village you come to is Rodley, about five and a half miles from Office Lock. The next stretch of walking is mostly rural, with the canal sweeping round wooded hillsides and passing the maintenance yard at Apperley Bridge. A good target for a first day's walk is Shipley, about thirteen miles from the centre of Leeds. Bridge 208 in Shipley marks the junction with the old Bradford Canal, long filled in. Much of Shipley's past prosperity derived from the canal. From here Leeds is readily accessible by train or bus.

The next few miles hold particular interest. First comes the industrial village of Saltaire, planned and built by the wealthy millowner Sir Titus Salt in the 1850s to house his workers. He provided them with all amenities available at that time except for a public house, and Saltaire still has none. Two miles further on is the Dowley Gap staircase pair of locks; then you enter the industrial town of Bingley with its two spectacular lock staircases; first the three-rise and then the famous five-rise, one of the 'wonders of the waterways'. Study the instructions

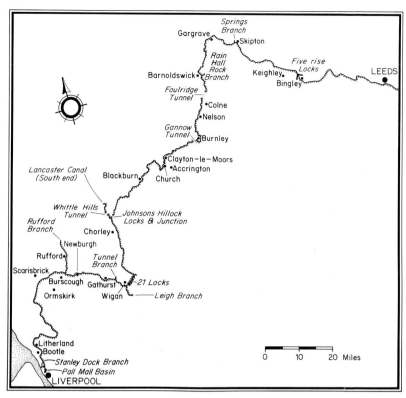

Map 15 The Leeds & Liverpool Canal

outside the lock-keeper's house and see if you can understand their working. Better still, wait until you can watch a boat attempting the passage—and watch, if it is a first-timer, with a sympathetic eye.

You are now over 300ft above sea level and there are no more locks for a further 16 miles, though for entertainment you may encounter boat crews struggling with the many swing bridges along this section; some of them are notoriously difficult to shift. It might be advisable, unless you are especially energetic, to end this day's walk by the Stockbridge swing bridge, number 197, from where it is a mile to Keighley along the A650. At Keighley Station is the Worth Valley Railway with five miles of track to Haworth operated by steam trains, a fascinating excursion if you have time in hand. There is a fine collection of locomotives on this line.

138

Back on the towpath, the next few miles are pleasant enough but not especially spectacular. The small industrial town of Silsden is some three miles further on; note the many stone-built canalside warehouses. In another two miles is Kildwick, a village set on a steep hillside, with attractive stone cottages and an awesome church. The hills stretch away into the distance while close to the canal the A629 keeps you company if the weather is bad and you wish to escape. A further two hours walking brings you to Skipton, a busy little town popular with tourists in summer. The canal is very close to the centre and Skipton with its many amenities, including excellent shops, a castle, and good bus and train services, is a suitable place to break your canalside journey. Explore the short Springs Branch of the canal which leads to quarries beneath the castle and note how here the canal, though no longer a commercial highway, is still an integral part of the town's life.

Skipton calls itself, with some justice, the 'Gateway to the Dales'; it is also the gateway to one of the finest lengths of rural canalscape in the country. It is a gentle 5 miles to Gargrave, apart from a few yards outside Skipton where the towpath is now part of the A59 main road, and although road and railway are not far away it is surprisingly quiet and peaceful. The River Aire, clean and narrow, continues to keep you company until, to the west of Gargrave, it ducks under the canal and heads away northwards for good. As you approach Gargrave you come to the end of the sixteen mile pound that began at Bingley; six locks lift the canal as it rounds the northern boundary of the village. You will already have noted the variety of paddle gear on the Leeds & Liverpool locks; here again there are interesting examples as well as some attractive bridges. Gargrave itself, intersected by the Aire, is a handsome village; from here you can catch a bus to Malham to explore the cove and tarn and appreciate the drama of Gordale Scar.

The canal is now at its most northerly point. Leaving the village you turn southwards for Banknewton locks, 2 miles away. This is a flight of six, recently refurbished and with a wide gravelled towpath. The Yorkshire Dales hire cruisers wharf is a model of its kind. At some of the locks there are iron hooks to assist in controlling the towing lines in times past.

Now you are beginning the most isolated and spectacular

On the Banknewton flight, Leeds & Liverpool Canal *(R. Russell)*

section of your walk. In the next few miles the canal winds around the contours, and although you might be tempted to leave the towpath and cut across some of the bends it is worth staying beside the canal, if time allows, to enjoy the changing views as you walk. You see a few small farmhouses and cottages nestling between rocky hillocks with the hills rising into mountains in the distance. At East Marton there is a bridge carrying the A59 across the canal, a unique structure with one arch built on top of the original one when the road approach was altered to improve visibility. Beside the bridge is The Cross Keys Inn and the towpath itself here is part of the Pennine Way. It is worth knowing that The Cross Keys is the only pub between Gargrave and the outskirts of Barnoldswick, some four miles further on.

South of East Marton there is another splendid scenic walk with only one minor road crossing to remind you of the bustling modern world. Next come the three Greenberfield locks, impressive in their upland setting; these replaced a three-rise staircase in 1820 and you may detect evidence of the old channel and bridge. The locks lift the canal to its summit level; the building by the lock-keeper's cottage controls the water supply to the summit from Winterburn. Another mile brings you to the edge of Barnoldswick, its centre about half a mile along the road from Bridge 153.

Now you are nearing the end of the finest rural section of the walk. South of Barnoldswick is Salterforth with The Anchor beside the canal; then two miles onwards the canal enters the 1,640yd tunnel at Foulridge, just over the Lancashire border. As there is no towpath you have to divert through the village, calling perhaps at The Hole in the Wall to study the newspaper cuttings telling the story of Buttercup, the cow who swam through the tunnel in 1912. The summit level ends shortly after you regain the towpath when the seven Barrowford locks begin the descent to Liverpool.

Greenberfield Locks on the Leeds & Liverpool: note the disused channel by the white house on the right *(British Waterways Board)*

From here on, a further 80 miles of walking is available through industrial Lancashire, with Nelson, Burnley, Blackburn, Wigan and Liverpool itself on your route. Except in Liverpool, access to the towpath is no problem, and from it you can obtain a fascinating picture of what is happening—and has happened—in industrial Lancashire. There are rural stretches as well, the most attractive being the few miles either side of the estate village of Withnell Fold, about five miles south-west of Blackburn.

Of the industrial stretches of canal, the route through Burnley is exceptional. This includes the 559yd Gannow Tunnel, through which there is no towpath, and a massive embankment, almost a mile long, taking the canal across the centre of the town some 60ft above street level. In earlier years this embankment formed the boundary of the built-up town centre, but in the later nineteenth century Burnley expanded to the east. There are about five miles of towpath walking here, with a great deal to see. Luckily the Burnley Teachers' Centre has produced a detailed and authoritative guide to the towpath, *Along t'Cut,* obtainable in the town or by post; this is indispensable if you want to get the most out of your walk.

Blackburn has nothing to match Burnley's embankment but it does have a flight of six locks not far from the town centre, which itself has been rebuilt in recent years so that it is virtually indistinguishable from so many other town centres that once enjoyed their own character and idiosyncrasies. If you happen to be in the neighbourhood it is worth walking the towpath; but, given the choice, a walk through Burnley would be preferable. To my knowledge there is no comparable guide to Blackburn's towpath either.

The next major industrial centre is Wigan, a vigorous and long-established industrial town built on a hillside down which the canal descends through twenty-three locks. The waterway potential of Wigan has been enhanced by the 1983 National Rally of Boats. You are likely to be accompanied on the towpath by members of boats' crews battling their way up or down the flight. There are three pubs near the top of the flight and it is worth pausing to survey the industrial landscape. Look for the site of Wigan Pier, opposite warehouses and the British Waterways Board's offices. A branch to Leigh leaves the canal near the

142

bottom lock; also nearby is the River Douglas, once navigable up to Wigan. There was a lock into the river near the M6 crossing and Dean locks, about three miles from Wigan centre.

There are 35 miles of canal between Wigan and the terminus by the sugar refinery in Liverpool; anyone walking this stretch would do well to bring out his own towpath guide to encourage others. Always remember that if walkers do not use the tow-paths, and boats fail to use the canals, there may come a time when neither canal nor towpath will be there to be used by any-one at all.

22 THE MONTGOMERYSHIRE
CANAL · Ronald Russell *(33 miles)*

Stretching 33 miles into Wales to search out limestone and wool, the Montgomeryshire Canal traverses beautiful countryside, much of it in the Upper Severn valley. The canal—usually known as the Montgomery or Monty for short—was built in stages from a junction with what is today known as the Llangollen Canal at Welsh Frankton to the wool town of Newtown. In 1936, following a breach in the bank at Welsh Frankton, it was closed by its then owners, the London, Midland & Scottish Railway, and was officially abandoned eight years later. However, despite the destruction of many road bridges and the obliteration of the topmost two miles, hope for its eventual reopening has never died. Since the awakening of interest in the leisure and recreational possibilities of inland waterways, the Montgomery has been in the forefront of schemes for restoration. Work began in earnest in 1969 and has continued, in fits and starts, until some 7½ miles have been made navigable and proposals for the destruction of further lengths and bridges have been defeated. It is entirely volunteers who have kept the canal's prospects alive but their efforts are now strengthened by its owners, the British Waterways Board, the Countryside Commission and the Prince of Wales' Committee. Walking the towpath, you will be able to judge for yourself the size of the task that lies ahead and the achievements that have already been accomplished.

The towpath is walkable almost throughout, although a few short diversions are necessary, for instance where the canal has been piped for a short distance. While the going may not always be even or regular, efforts are being made to improve the towpath and there is no intention of deterring walkers from using it. Your main problem may be how to plan your walk as the northernmost section of the canal is especially remote and public transport elsewhere, although it exists, is infrequent. The small town of Ellesmere is an extra five miles towpath walk from Welsh Frankton and the A495 between Ellesmere and Oswestry passes just over a mile from the junction. The ideal solution is to

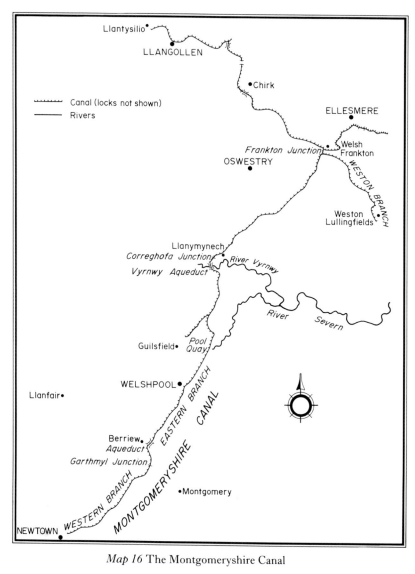

Map 16 The Montgomeryshire Canal

have a friendly boat-owner pick you up or drop you at Welsh
Frankton on his way to or from Llangollen.

Some of the old buildings still exist around Welsh Frankton
locks, including a toll-house, a lock-keeper's cottage and the
former Canal Tavern, now a private house. Much evidence of

the trading activity has disappeared but parts of Beech's boatyard can be found below the locks. A few hundred yards past the bottom lock by Lockgate Bridge you will see an arm leading off to the east. This is the beginning of the derelict Weston Branch, originally intended to be part of a main line canal between Chester and Shrewsbury. It leads, much of it indiscernible, across fields to its terminus at Westonwharf, 5 miles away. Should you venture there you will find many of the original buildings still standing around the canal basin; only the people, water and boats are missing.

Continuing southwards along the line of the Montgomery, look for evidence of the 1936 breach in the opposite bank. It is nearly three miles between roads here and only one major canal artefact to see: the three-arched aqueduct over the River Perry, in shaky and somewhat dangerous condition. A mile along you come to the remains of Rednal boneworks, once served by the canal; then there is a railway bridge as the canal runs up alongside a minor road by the site of Rednal Wharf and an unusual little warehouse built in mock-Elizabethan style that was connected with the packet boat service from Newtown which terminated here for the transfer of passengers to the railway. Now there is a straight stretch of nearly a mile to the A5 crossing at Queen's Head where you can distinguish the site of the wharf although the canal is culverted beneath the main road. You are now just over four miles from the junction.

If you are using Oswestry as a base, Queen's Head is an obvious place at which to begin your walk as the main road from Oswestry, the A4083, meets the A5 very close to the canal. As you continue south-westward along the towpath you come in less than a mile to Aston locks, with remnants of a lock-keeper's cottage and, in the reeds, an ice-breaker. Two miles from Queen's Head is Maesbury Marsh, a canal settlement where several boatmen used to live. Here were two wharves, one either side of the bridge, and a boneworks, of which the chimney remains. The Navigation Inn, fortunately, is still functioning. From Maesbury Mill ran the last regular narrow boat service on the canal; this ceased operating in 1932 when it became uneconomic for the Peate family, owners of both mill and boats, to use the canal because of silting up. The most famous narrow boat of all, L. T. C. Rolt's *Cressy*, was once owned by Peates and worked on the Montgomery Canal.

The country you continue to walk through was once busy with industry, with many mines, brickworks and mills. A wharf by Bridge 82 was served by a horse-drawn tramway during much of the nineteenth century, connecting the canal with nearby collieries. The canal itself here is mostly in poor condition but there are no problems in following the towpath. At Redwith, where the B4396 crosses, there is one surviving wall of a wharf and a bank of lime kilns. Crickheath, three-quarters of a mile further on, has more substantial relics including a lengthsman's cottage, shed and a house that was once a pub. Another tramway terminated by the wharf wall, used for transporting limestone in the canal's earlier days.

A further 1¼ miles brings you to Pant; any of the minor roads crossing your path will take you quickly to the A483 to Oswestry, 4 miles away. By Bridge 88 there was another limestone wharf served by a tramway that used the small bridge hole. It may be best to take the parallel minor road on the east side of the canal between here and Bridge 90 to avoid barbed wire and other obstacles. By Bridge 90 there are lime kilns and, if you climb the hill behind the café, you can find a haulage drum that once operated a tramway up and down the hill. It is just over a mile from Pant to Llanymynech, another limestone loading and burning centre. On arrival you can pause for refreshment in The Dolphin; you have covered 10½ miles from Welsh Frankton.

Continuing from Llanymynech, you pass Walls Bridge, site of another wharf, and Wern Bridge, where an aqueduct crosses the disused railway line. In a mile are Carreghofa locks, gradually being restored by volunteers from the Shropshire Union Canal Society. Here was the junction between the Ellesmere and Montgomeryshire canals as they were originally built; many of the old buildings survive including the wharfinger's office by the top lock and a lock-keeper's cottage below. The side pound of water, used to operate the bottom lock, is fed by the River Tanat.

The next bridge, number 96, Williams Bridge, is notorious among canal restorers since in 1980, despite lively and frequent protests, it was flattened by Powys County Council. The council say that this barrier to through restoration is temporary, but only time will tell. Near Williams Bridge is the heavy and leaky Vyrnwy Aqueduct, held together by the iron-work inserted by the engineer G. W. Buck some thirty years after it was built.

For the next 3 miles you are heading southwards, and from now on you are never far from the A483, convenient if you are dependent on a car to meet you during your walk. Look for evidence of wharves and warehouses close to the bridges; also note the lime kilns, frequent along this canal. By Maerdy Bridge, number 102, there was a dock and The Bell, now no longer a public house. Soon you will appreciate the problems presented by the recent building of a bypass, which crosses the canal on a lowered bridge; this means that the canal itself will have to be lowered by moving the position of the nearby lock if through navigation is to be achieved. The new road caused the demolition of the remains of wharves at Ardleen.

At the top of Burgedin locks the Guilsfield Branch forks off to the south-west. It is 2½ miles long and ends at Tyddin Basin, once quite busy with timber, where a few of the old buildings survive. It is easier to follow the branch by taking the B4392 road, which is close to it for all its length. The branch itself is now a nature reserve.

Back alongside the main line you may be lucky enough to see a boat on the move, as this stretch has been restored as far as Welshpool, six miles away. Bridge 106 at The Wern is the lowest point on the canal; clay from a pit here was and is used for the canal, and the canal company had a brickyard nearby. Look also for the New Cut, taking away surplus water to the Severn. You no longer enjoy the feeling of remoteness as the canal continues close to the busy main road, but the wooded countryside is pleasant compensation. You pass a couple of bridges and locks; then about six hundred yards after Crowther Hall Lock you come to Quay House, a warehouse and another lock, Pool Quay.

There is not much about Pool Quay itself to recall its history, but the loop of the Severn on the far side of the main road was the river's old head of navigation. The Severn was navigable to Pool Quay in the first half of the nineteenth century for vessels up to thirty tons and for some years goods from Welshpool were transhipped here for the river ports of Worcester and Gloucester. The ancient weir which enabled the river to be navigated was destroyed by floods in 1881. Much of Welshpool's earlier prosperity depended on Pool Quay.

Another hour's good walking brings you to Welshpool, passing in turn the aptly named Abbey Heave-Up Bridge and Moors Lift-Up Bridge. Near the first of these and between the main road and the river was once Strata Marcella Abbey, whose monks first built the weir, demolished in 1536. After the second bridge you come to Buttington Wharf, recently landscaped and with its bank of lime kilns carefully preserved. A narrow boat for the disabled is moored at Buttington; it was launched by Prince Charles in 1976, further evidence of the interest the Prince and his committee take in the Montgomery Canal. The lowered bridge you arrive at next is Gallows Tree Bank Bridge, another apt name, and then you are entering Welshpool, perhaps looking forward to a good night's sleep.

You enter the town passing first the remains of the Powysland Factory, originally a tweed and flannel mill and later an ordnance factory in World War I, and the yards of The Powis Arms and The Queen's Head, both at one time housing trades and activities connected with the canal. Between the Mill Lane and Severn Street bridges is a cast-iron aqueduct over the Lledan Brook and the sites of wharves and warehouses, one of the latter being used by the British Waterways Board staff today. Beyond Severn Street Bridge is the town basin, with wharves, warehouse and lock, restored over ten years ago, a place famous in the history of canal restoration as this length was nearly lost to a road scheme in 1969. You leave Welshpool between Hollybush Wharf and the old Shropshire Union Repair Yard and head southwards alongside the A483 with a further thirteen miles to go. Powis Castle Park is to the west; the Earls of Powis were much involved with the Montgomery and the major canals in the region; the products of their mills and quarries formed a large proportion of the waterways' traffic. Timber was loaded by Whitehouse Bridge, number 120, and the Estate Yard was busy with a watermill, boneyard and smithy.

The main road crosses the canal at Whitehouse Bridge and the next 3 miles comprise one of the most interesting stretches of the walk. The area around Belan locks is a microcosm of the

Montgomery: a pair of locks, one either side of a bridge, with a cottage by the lower, splendid cast-iron ground paddle gear (of which you will already have seen some examples), a well-designed overflow weir and the hulls of two canal craft, a fly boat and a coal boat, rotting amongst the reeds. There is also a bank of lime kilns, reputedly the busiest on the canal; and nearby is a reminder of more ancient days: the line of a Roman road on its way to a crossing of the Severn guarded by a fort at Forden. A few hundred yards along is Belan School, built of stone brought by canal from Welshpool, whose children enjoyed boat outings on the Montgomery for many decades.

At Brithdir, 2 miles from Belan, where the A483 almost touches the canal is The Horseshoes Inn, where there used to be a smithy in the yard, a bank of kilns and a wharf and storehouse near the lock, with its keeper's house. South of the bridge a cast-iron aqueduct with ornamental railings takes the canal over the Luggy; this replaced a masonry aqueduct in 1820. Rectory Lock comes in just under a mile, followed by Berriew Bridge, more warehouse and wharf sites, and Berriew Aqueduct over the Rhiw, built by the Dadfords, father and son, the canal's first engineers, in 1797 and extensively rebuilt in 1889. The canal is now piped across.

Most, if not all, of the evidence of wharves, lime kilns and a dry dock by Bridge 129 has gone, although the Jerusalem Chapel Assembly Rooms survive. A further half-mile brings you to Garthmyl and the A483, a useful dropping or pick-up point for your walk.

Garthmyl is important in the canal's history as it was here that the Eastern and Western branches joined. The canal ended at this point in 1797; several wharves were built, three banks of lime kilns and a number of associated buildings. With the canal's prosperity apparently established, the Western extension was begun in 1815 and opened in 1821 to Newtown; but the good years of trading were soon over and both branches were merged in the Shropshire Union takeover in 1850. The old road overbridge now stands isolated and parallel to the main road which has squashed the Montgomery beneath it. You can pause and reflect on all this in The Nag's Head Inn.

Another 7½ miles brings you to Newtown with the main road and the Severn never far away, the road crossing the canal

Aqueduct over the Bechan Brook, Montgomeryshire Canal *(R. Russell)*

three times. Indeed the proximity of the road does not enhance this stretch and as there is nothing of special interest on the next 2½ miles you will lose little by omitting them if you are doing the walk in stages. At Brynderwen the road crosses for the last time and thenceforth is further away; this is a good point to resume the towpath. Here was a coal wharf, and a typical Shropshire Union warehouse still stands.

The Abermule bypass has eliminated the towpath, among other things, but the way ahead is easy to find. Then there are two more locks, Byles and Newhouse, and a further three-quarters of a mile brings you to one of the canal's more elegant structures, a three-arch aqueduct of sandstone across the Bechan Brook. Aberbechan itself was busy with canal trade, mainly coal and lime. The road bridge across the canal was made of four cast-iron beams from the Brymbo Works, which provided much of the iron for the canal's artefacts.

The watered (or damp) channel of the canal ends at Freestone Lock, the next one along. The remaining 2 miles now belong to the Severn–Trent Water Authority and the towpath walk is currently being improved and extended into Newtown. If you follow the feeder by the lock you come to the Severn and a large curved weir with salmon ladder and sluices and you can walk along the river bank around the sewage works to pick up the canal line again. This leads you past Llanllwchaiarn Church, then the path becomes converted into a private drive. A stone garage by the house this leads to, bearing the date 1860, was at one time the engine house for a water pump operated by a water-wheel, with the engine in reserve. This was built by G. W. Buck to raise water from the Severn to the top section of canal, instead of cutting a feeder which would have affected the supply to the mills of Newtown.

On the approach to Newtown a flood bank partly obscures the canal line but you can follow this between mills once served by the canal. After the Central Dairies you cross the canal bridge on Dolafon Road, turn left by The Waggon and Horses and arrive at the site of Newtown Basin behind a row of wharfingers' cottages. A very useful sketch map of Newtown Basin in 1840 can be found in leaflet 4 of a series entitled *About the Montgomery Canal* prepared as part of a Manpower Services Commission STEP scheme. The four leaflets, together with others dealing with aspects of the canal in Welshpool, can be obtained from 2 Canal Yard, Welshpool. Not only am I grateful to their authors for allowing me to make much use of their work in this description, but I am glad to recommend the leaflets as models of their kind, beautifully presented and illustrated and containing a wealth of information about the canal and the surrounding area. Anyone walking the towpath—and this is one of the best of the longer canalside walks—will find these leaflets indispensable.

BIBLIOGRAPHY

Bick, David. *The Hereford & Gloucester Canal* (The Pound House, 1979)

Biddle, Gordon. *Lancashire Waterways* (Dalesman, 1980)

Braithwaite, Lewis. *Canals in Towns* (A. & C. Black, 1976)

British Waterways Board. 'A Walk on the Wildside' (British Waterways Board)

——'London Canals: recreational use of towing paths'. Recreation Planning Working Paper 5 (British Waterways Board, 1979)

——*London's Canal Walks* (British Waterways Board, 1983; free on request)

——'Monmouthshire & Brecon Canal: towing-path user survey' Recreation Planning Research Paper 9 (British Waterways Board, 1980)

Broadbridge, S. R. *The Birmingham Canal Navigations* (David & Charles, 1974)

Burnley Teachers' Centre. *Along t'Cut* (Lancashire County Library, 1977)

Chaplin, T. *The Narrow Boat Book* (Whittet Books, 1978)

——*Short History of the Narrow Boat* (Shepperton Swan, 1979)

Chester-Brown, R. *The Other Sixty Miles* (Birmingham Canal Navigation Society, 1981)

Clew, Kenneth. *The Dorset & Somerset Canal* (David & Charles, 1971)

——*The Kennet & Avon Canal,* 2nd edn (David & Charles, 1973)

——*The Somersetshire Coal Canal and Railways* (David & Charles, 1970)

——*Wessex Waterway* (Moonraker Press, 1978)

Compton, H. *The Oxford Canal* (David & Charles, 1977)

Dalby, L. J. *The Canal at Newbury* (Kennet & Avon Canal Trust)

——*The Wiltshire & Berkshire Canal* (Oakwood Press, 1971)

Denney, M. *London's Waterways* (Batsford, 1977)

Droitwich Canal Trust. *Towpath Guide to the Droitwich Canal* (Droitwich Canal Trust)

Edwards, L. A. *Inland Waterways of Great Britain,* 5th edn (Imray, Laurie, Norie & Wilson, 1972)

Faulkner, A. H. *The Grand Junction Canal* (David & Charles, 1972)

Gagg, J. *Observer's Book of Canals* (Frederick Warne, 1982)

Hadfield, Charles. *British Canals,* 7th edition (David & Charles, 1984)

——*The Canals of the West Midlands* (David & Charles, 1978)

Handford, Michael. *The Stroudwater Canal* (Alan Sutton, 1979)

——and Viner, David. *A Towpath Guide to the Stroudwater, Thames & Severn Canals* (Alan Sutton, 1983)

Hanson, Harry. *Canal People* (David & Charles, 1978)

Harris, Helen. *The Grand Western Canal* (David & Charles, 1973)

——and Ellis, Monica. *The Bude Canal* (David & Charles, 1972)

Hodges, H. *A Guide to the Worcester & Birmingham Canal* (Worcester & Birmingham Canal Society, 1981)

Household, H. *The Thames & Severn Canal* (David & Charles, 1969)

Huddersfield Canal Society. *The Huddersfield Canal Towpath Guide* (Huddersfield Canal Society, 1981)

Lamb, Brian. *The Peak Forest Canal and Tramway* (Inland Waterways Protection Society, 1976)

Langford, J. I. *The Staffordshire & Worcestershire Canal Towpath Guide* (Goose & Son, 1974)

Lewery, A. J. *Narrow Boat Painting* (David & Charles, 1974)

Lindsay, J. *The Trent & Mersey Canal* (David & Charles, 1979)

Owen, D. E. *Canals to Manchester* (Manchester University Press, 1977)

——*Cheshire Waterways* (Dalesman, 1979)

Manpower Services Commission. *About the Montgomery Canal* (HMSO, 1981)

McKnight, H. *The Shell Book of Inland Waterways,* 2nd edn (David & Charles, 1981)

Paget-Tomlinson, E. W. *The Complete Book of Canal and River Navigations* (Waine Research, 1978)

——*Britain's Canal and River Craft* (Moorland, 1979)

Phillips, John. *History of Inland Navigation* (David & Charles, 1970; first published 1792)

Pratt, D. *Discovering London's Canals* (Shire Publications, 1977)

Rolt, L. T. C. *The Inland Waterways of England* (Allen & Unwin, 1950)

——*Narrow Boat* (Eyre Methuen, 1944)

——*Navigable Waterways* (Longman, 1969)

Russell, Ronald. *Discovering Lost Canals* (Shire Publications, 1975)

——*Lost Canals and Waterways of Britain* (David & Charles, 1982)

Sheffield City Museums. *Navigation: the Story of the Sheffield to Tinsley Canal* (Sheffield City Museums, 1980)

154

Smith, D. T. *Canal Boats and Boaters* (Hugh Evelyn, 1973)

Smith, P. L. *Yorkshire Waterways* (Dalesman, 1978)

Spencer, H. *London's Canal* (GLC, 1969)

Stevens, P. A. *The Leicester Line* (David & Charles, 1972)

Stevens, R. A. *The Brecknock & Abergavenny and Monmouthshire Canals* (Goose & Son, 1974)

Stevenson, P. *The Nutbrook Canal* (David & Charles, 1971)

Thurston, E. Temple. *The Flower of Gloster* (David & Charles, 1968; first published 1911)

Vine, P. A.L. *London's Lost Route to Basingstoke* (David & Charles, 1969)

——*London's Lost Route to the Sea,* 3rd edn (David & Charles, 1973)

——*The Royal Military Canal* (David & Charles, 1972)

Waterspace Amenity Commission. 'The Potential of Towpaths as Waterside Footpaths' (WSAC, 1977)

'Waterways World', *The Staffordshire & Worcestershire Canal* (1981)

——*Guide to the South Oxford Canal* (1981)

Wey & Arun Canal Trust. *Wey–South Path* (Wey & Arun Canal Trust)

Wilson, Robert. *Life Afloat* (Robert Wilson, 1976)

USEFUL ADDRESSES

The Boat Museum, Ellesmere Port, Cheshire L65 4EF

British Waterways Board, Melbury House, Melbury Terrace, London NW1 6JX

Caldon Canal Society (W. G. Myatt), Long Barrow, Butterton, Newcastle, Staffs

Droitwich Canals Trust, 1 Hampton Road, Droitwich, Worcs WR9 8PN

Forth & Clyde Canal Society (Jerry Cross), 20 Crosshill Avenue, Crosshill, Glasgow G42

Herefordshire & Gloucestershire Canal Society (J. Dunn), Old Deanery House, Cathedral Close, Hereford

Huddersfield Canal Society, (R. A. Dewey), 28 Cinderhills Road, Holmfirth, Huddersfield HF7 1EH

Inland Waterways Association, 114 Regent's Park Road, London NW1 8UQ

Inland Waterways Protection Society (Ian Edgar), The Cottage, 69 Ivy Road, Macclesfield SK11 8QN

Kennet & Avon Canal Trust (P. Collins), Devizes Wharf, Couch Lane, Devizes, Wilts.

Linlithgow Union Canal Society, 6 Royal Terrace, Linlithgow, W. Lothian

Macclesfield Canal Society, 4 Endon Drive, Brown Lees, Biddulph, Staffs

National Bus Company, 25 New Street Square, London EC4A 3AP

The National Trust, 36 Queen Anne's Gate, London SW1

Peak Forest Canal Society (D. L. Brown), 26 Delamere Street, Openshaw, Manchester 11

Railway & Canal Historical Society (R. E. Kilsby, Secretary), Banestree, Jacobs Well Road, Jacobs Well, Guildford, Surrey GU4 7PA.

Ramblers' Association, 15 Wandsworth Road, London SW8 2LJ

Sheffield Canal Society (W. R. Probert), 8 Main Road, Holmesfield, Sheffield

Staffs & Worcs Canal Society (A. Emuss), 165 Canal Side, Lower Whittington, Kinver, Staffs DY7 6NU

Stroudwater, Thames & Severn Canal Trust, 1 Riveredge, Framilode, Glos.

Trent & Mersey Canal Society (H. Arnold), 26 Chaseview Road, Alrewas, Burton-on-Trent, Staffs DE13 7EL

Waterways Museum, Stoke Bruerne, Towcester, Northants

Waterways World (monthly magazine, publishers of canal guides, book supply services) Kottingham House, Dale Street, Burton-on-Trent, Staffs DE14 3TD

Wilts & Berks Canal Amenity Society (P. H. Boyce) 31A Stafford Street, Swindon, Wilts SN1 3PH

Worcester & Birmingham Canal Society (Mrs R. Ward), 71 Birmingham Road, Alvechurch, Birmingham B48 7TD

INDEX

The numbers in italic refer to illustrations